"As you sent me into the world, so I have
sent them into the world."

John 17:18

Becoming Amish

*A family's search for faith,
community and purpose*

by Jeff Smith

Dance Hall Press

Published by Dance Hall Press, LLC
5220 South Good Harbor Trail
Cedar, Michigan 49621

First published in the United States of America by
Dance Hall Press, LLC.

Library of Congress Control Number: 2016903695

ISBN: 978-0-9973733-0-1

Printed in the United States of America

Cover and book design by Robert Wilcox.
Cover photograph by Jeffrey David Smith

Becoming Amish began as a magazine article in the November 2009
issue of *Traverse, Northern Michigan's Magazine.* Portions of the article are
included here with permission of the magazine's publisher, MyNorth Media.

BecomingAmish.net

For Joyce Moser, Marie Beaghan and
Peggy Gottschalk, moms who raised Bill,
Tricia and Jeff in the neighborhoods
of Livonia, Michigan.

{CONTENTS}

Meeting
Bill and Tricia

I MET BILL MOSER WHEN HE WAS FOUR YEARS OLD. I was four years old too. We lived three houses apart in a suburb of Detroit called Livonia. Our subdivision was a new one, and most of the yards were still dirt when we met, which is perfect if you're four. We made twisting roadways in the dirt and pushed Matchbox cars around. Like any four-year-olds rich in dirt, we built towns, and if we wanted a lake in our little town, we'd just dig one and fill it with the garden hose and not get in trouble for digging a hole in the yard. A lot of fun ended when our parents installed sod.

If it's possible for a place to be extreme middle class, Livonia was it back then. No visible poor people. No visible rich people. "Ethnic people" meant neighbors whose grandparents had come from Italy or Ireland or the Ukraine, but there were no accents that I recall. On International Food Day at Hull Elementary School, where Bill and I attended, we ate things like lasagna and Polish sausage. I remember something Mexican, like maybe enchiladas, but I don't remember any Mexican people in Hull Elementary, because we definitely didn't see brown people in Livonia, though Detroit, one of the most African-American cities in the nation, was just ten minutes away. Even today, Livonia has the highest percentage of Caucasians of any city with more than 100,000 residents in the United States—the whitest big town in America.

Sometimes I wonder if the homogeneous nature of our town, the monoculture, inspired Bill's curiosity about other people, his desire to look into other worlds and understand and adopt the good that was there. Don't know, but something that makes me think so is Bill was the first person I knew who was really into soul music. Not in a "trying to be a brother" sort of way, but just in a natural "I'm really into this sound" sort of way.

One time, when we were sixteen, he bought us tickets to a Marvin Gaye concert at Olympia Stadium, in a dilapidated neighborhood of Detroit. We each took dates. This was 1974; the Detroit race riots were just seven years behind us. The racial divide was perhaps greater than ever, and people in Livonia were afraid to go into Detroit. But Bill loved the music, and he intuitively understood that people getting together for a Marvin Gaye concert—"How Sweet It Is to Be Loved by You" and "Let's Get It On"—were looking to make love not problems. And his sixteen-year-old's instinct proved right. I remember seeing about ten white people in the sold-out arena of 15,000, and everybody went out of their way to make us feel welcome.

Now follow along as we fast-forward. Bill goes to University of Detroit to study architecture. He graduates. Bill marries Tricia, the Catholic girl he went to the Marvin Gaye concert with. She, by now, is an occupational therapist, having graduated from Wayne State University. I am the best man in the wedding. Bill and Tricia move into Indian Village, the hippest neighborhood in Detroit, start driving a BMW and party with Detroiters they later call "artsy." Back in the 1980s, people would have labeled Bill and Tricia as yuppies. When my wife and I get married a few years after Bill and Tricia's wedding, Bill is my best man; Tricia is a bridesmaid.

Now five years further, Bill and Tricia are living in Grosse Pointe Park. Bill has a prominent role in designing a building in the exclusive downtown of Birmingham, Michigan. Soon, he starts his own construction-design company. The couple also starts to become increasingly religious, and they join an evangelical church.

Meanwhile, my wife and I have moved to Minneapolis. We do not become increasingly religious. On one visit back to Michigan, we meet the Mosers at their longtime family cabin in Gladwin. I bring a guitar and play some songs, including a lively number that Bill seems to like. "What's the name of that one?" he asks.

"Friend of the Devil," I say. "By the Grateful Dead."

A disapproving look crosses Tricia's face, and I see her eyes locking with Bill's for a longish moment. An awkward silence follows. I feel an urge to explain, to say, "hey, man, it's just a song," but I don't. After that weekend, we seem to stay in touch with the Mosers less and less, and due to place and lifestyle, we drift apart.

Skip ahead to 1998. My family has by now moved back to Michigan, to a northern Great Lakes harbor town called Traverse City. We haven't talked to the Mosers in at least a few years, and we did not track them down to tell them we were back in the state. But one day I get a call at work from Tricia inviting us to visit their small farm near Ovid, in mid-Michigan farm country twenty miles north of the state capital of Lansing. It turns out I'll be passing nearby in a few days on my way to Detroit Metropolitan Airport to pick up my two oldest children, who are returning from visiting friends in Minneapolis. It is the height of summer, crazy busy, but a short visit? Sure. I pull off the highway, steer down dirt roads and pull up to the house.

I get out of my car and stand for a moment in the lush July dusk, pausing to process what's in front of me. A horse grazes in a small paddock. Chest-high grasses with seed-tops tinged in purple twilight fill a low swale. An especially orangey glow illuminates the house windows. I hear quiet. I feel peace. But also my mind is spinning, because nowhere do I see a car, and in the driveway there stands a black buggy, as in horse and buggy.

I knock on the door, and Bill answers with Tricia and his six children crowded round. Bill has a beard, suspenders, plain blue denim pants and shirt. Tricia wears a cap, an ankle-length dress. The children dress likewise. Bill and I hug. Tricia and I hug. A self-conscious smile crosses Bill's face. "Well," he says, "do you think we've gone crazy?"

I like to think of the Mosers as an all-American family. That probably sounds silly; after all, what could be less all-American than joining a community that holds as one of its most important beliefs the notion that they should actively separate from general society. But still, that's how I think of them, and in part, I do mean all-American in the standard way. There's Bill the dad and Tricia the mom. They have raised five boys and one girl. They are homeowners. They are business owners. They are farmers. They are churchgoers. They are community members who help out, pitch in, donate money and time and spiritual support. They pay taxes. They wonder about global warming, the safety of industrial-scale food, moral decline, the divorce rate and drug abuse.

But I also mean all-American in another way, in the way that means taking advantage of American rights to pursue the faith of your choice, to shape your own views, to live the life you feel is most rewarding for yourself and your family. Sure, the Mosers never have football on the big-screen TV, a thirty-rack of Pabst handy and a steaming platter of barbecued chicken wings on the coffee table, but in more important ways, the Mosers are the most all-American people I know because they have pursued their convictions and led the purposeful life that our Bill of Rights allows.

I wanted to write this book because the more I learned about the Mosers' journey, the more I felt it offered insightful counterpoint to life in today's America. Their journey began as a journey of faith. But as anybody who has ever seen even a photo of an Amish person can guess, the journey also involves a constellation of choices related to community and vocation and education and dress and transportation and technology and more. The more I learned about those choices, the more I became fascinated by how such a purposeful approach to life led to a richness that many in mainstream society would envy.

I was also struck by how the Mosers' decisions and the community's decisions were based on principles that defy what we in general society would call political ideological boundaries. The Amish act in ways that are extremely conservative and extremely liberal all at the same time. They would lose liberals with their give-no-ground, no-exceptions opposition to abortion, homosexuality and divorce. They would lose conservatives by refusing to fight in war. They would endear themselves to conservatives by rejecting government assistance—even to the point of denying themselves Social Security and Medicare checks they are eligible for. But they would endear themselves to the social-minded by gathering in a commune-like act to build a house for a member at no cost for labor, or sending word out through their churches to raise money for treating a cancer patient. The Amish would gain favor among fiscal conservatives by strongly promoting values like independence and financial responsibility, and they would gain favor among the social-minded by providing a remarkable network of support (free meals, subsidized housing …) for young people as they navigate their way through the often-difficult early adult years. They would appeal to the business-minded with their sense of entrepreneurialism. They would appeal to the social-minded with how they collectively support new business owners, giving advice and economic assistance to help new businesses take root and thrive. Of course, labels like "conservative" and "liberal" are from general society, and are not of much concern to the Amish. They know that their religion, family, community, employment—their lives, their choices—all unify, all make sense, all achieve singularity, when viewed as a straightforward interpretation of the teaching of Jesus.

This book about Bill and Tricia and their journey from general society to the world of the Amish is not intended as a discourse in "how to become Amish," nor is it a simplistic, rose-tinted, all gosh-and-shucks view of the plain lifestyle. ("Plain" is a common term describing the many, many groups who live low on the technology ladder.) The journey did not always go well for the Mosers, and they displayed great perseverance in sticking with it. The book is intended to function as a kind of mirror, a way to encourage readers to contemplate the choices they face, and consider a purposeful approach to their own lives.

I am not a religious person. More than once during the course of doing interviews and research for this book, that absence of religion has given people pause, because essentially all of the people I've spoken to hold faith in Jesus at the center of their lives. I can see them wondering why I would be interested in writing this book if I don't share their belief. Or I'm guessing they question whether I could be trusted to handle this important topic, the most important topic in the universe, I suspect they would say. As I explained it to Bill and Tricia and others along the way, I approached the story of the Mosers as I would approach a book about, say, Tibetan monks. I respect the choices they have made and I would hope to learn from those choices and be able to share the value of those choices with a reader, but just as I would not likely become a Tibetan monk, I am also not likely to become a devout Christian. "That is your path, but it is not likely to be my path," I told Bill and Tricia in the car one day.

There was a pause as they turned that over in their minds. "Well, we hope you understand that we hope one day you find what we have found," Bill said.

Just Married

Bill and Tricia Moser married in April 1981 in St. Paul of the Cross Monastery in Detroit. It was a turbulent time for people in Detroit, and while the phrase "a turbulent time" seems like it could apply to every nanosecond of life in Detroit since 1960, the spring of 1981 was especially troubled. White flight had pushed the city into a long decline, and the global recession of the early '80s—with its outsized impact on Michigan's carmakers—was hitting the Motor City full force that very month, pushing the unemployment rate to historic highs and lending momentum to Detroit's downward spiral. For just about any young, freshly married white couple in the Detroit Metro area, inner city Detroit would have been the very last place to choose to live.

But by the time they married, Bill and Tricia felt they had become a part of Detroit. Bill had pursued a five-year architecture degree at the University of Detroit, and he lived there in decaying neighborhoods the whole time. I remember Bill telling me that a pack of five large feral dogs lived beneath the porch of an abandoned house across the street from where he rented with his architecture school friends. They started a punk group—I think they played once—and for a name they paired the street name with dogs and came up with Santa Rosa Dogs in honor of the pack. As someone who had studied design and cities and neighborhoods, Bill became intrigued with the once-burgeoning city's decline, the city's potential and the city's vivid human drama.

For her part, Tricia had studied occupational therapy at Wayne State University, likewise a Detroit university surrounded by decaying neighborhoods, though she lived at home in Livonia during college. After she graduated, Tricia took a job working in an inner-city hospital called the Rehabilitation Institute of Detroit, where her patients were mostly elderly African Americans, but included high school gang members recovering from gunshot wounds.

It's fair to say that Bill and Tricia saw themselves as part of Detroit's hope. Young, educated, the skills to help a city, and a youthful belief in humanity's future. For people like this, in 1981, people willing to swim against the gushing tide of Detroit's white flight, the place to live was Indian Village, and that's where the Mosers went not long after they married.

Indian Village rose at the dawn of the 1900s, a direct expression of Detroit's own rise to global industrial stardom at the time, because this is where a clique of newly rich industrial captains chose to cluster. The best known was Henry Ford's only son Edsel, who purchased a home in 1917 and served as Ford president from 1919 to 1943. But one street west of Edsel lived Henry Leland, the man who founded both Lincoln and Cadillac, and one street east of Edsel lived the gentleman who founded Holley Carburetor. Another early Indian Village resident, and someone who certainly resonated with Bill, was Albert Kahn, the foremost industrial architect of the day and the man some call the Architect of Detroit. And there were many more, presidents and vice-presidents of manufacturing companies, partners of law firms and advertising agencies, every one a big gear in the mighty machine of early 1900s Detroit.

Somehow, over the decades, as the super rich moved on to the suburbs, there was always somebody else willing to move in to the aging industrial-era mansions and keep them in decent shape, so Indian Village remained an island of apparent opulence amid Detroit's decay. Leafy streets, groomed yards and mansions in a range of classic styles—gothic, prairie, Tudor, neo-Georgian, neo-Renaissance, neo-Colonial—all feeding Bill's architectural sense of self.

An art historian friend hooked up a rental—rare in the neighborhood—for Bill and Tricia, the second floor of a house on Seminole Street that was owned by a widow. "It felt right being an architect and driving down the street," Bill says. "People who lived there weren't extremely wealthy at that point, but they were renovating houses and were brave enough to live in Detroit's East Side and were committed to preserving the houses. That tied in with what I was all about, and I wanted to support that, be a part of that," he says.

Jobs in architecture were scarce in the recession, and Bill worked as a cook in a pancake place for about a year before finding a job, but the one he eventually landed seemed nearly storybook. He hired on at a dozen-person firm that worked from a hip, renovated carriage house near the Detroit River. Inside, the walls were stripped back to bare brick, a steel staircase slanted through midair, connecting the three floors. The space was open, airy, full of light and expressed a sleek, smart, industrial vibe. To me, it all seemed so Bill. The firm did a lot of work for the city, rehabbed Detroit's character-rich old buildings and renovated loft spaces. "It was interesting work if you liked the city, which I did," Bill says.

With two incomes, no kids and low rent, the Mosers had disposable money. And Bill in particular lived out his vision of spending life among what people now call the creative class. "We had an artsy lifestyle," he says. "There were a lot of restaurants and bars moving into the city's old buildings, and I was partying and going out to eat," he says. Between Bill's architecture friends and Tricia's friends from the hospital, the couple's social calendar stayed full. Bill drove to work in a Mitsubishi Montero, one of the first up-styled SUVs, which he bought over the phone from a dealer in Chicago. He was so taken by the design that, other than a photo, he never laid eyes on the Montero until he went to pick it up. Tricia drove a BMW. Bill told me once, "People think you drive a BMW because they're cool, but the real reason is they're the best driving machine made." Of course, at the time, neither one of us could have possibly known that eventually his driving machine of choice would be a horse and buggy.

Early Years
Together

T he Mosers were not rich by any means, but they had good starter jobs, lived in the right neighborhood, drove fashionable cars, hung out with successful friends. It's not an understatement to say the Mosers were living the life of their dreams. "It was a life I had envisioned, yes," Bill says. "But there was always this nagging thing. The dream was more exciting than the realization. I'd finish a project at work, and that was that, on to the next one." He figured Tricia was more satisfied in her life because she was working directly with people who had life-altering injuries. "More stressful, but also more rewarding," Bill says. "She was helping people, and that's the kind of person she is."

But Tricia was also unsatisfied, though for different reasons. The source of her nagging doubt was a spiritual questioning, a longing, a curiosity, even, you might say, a suspicion, which she could not quiet.

"I was going through a spiritual search," Tricia says. "And that part of my story is slow and gradual." Tricia's parents had raised their four daughters and son in a devout Catholic home, but Tricia's brother, during his high school years, had left Catholicism and moved to an evangelical faith, which endorsed a more one-to-one relationship with Jesus. Her brother was a couple of years younger, but Tricia looked up to him for his choice and was curious about it.

One of the things that most captivated her about her brother's life was the way he related to his Christian friends. His life was very social and their idea of partying was simply socializing alcohol-free in good clean fun. "His friends were so sweet and pure, and why? Because they had Christ in them. That was my first glimpse of that. When you realize somebody shares Christ with you, there is an immediate bond based on that and it gets deeper the more we go."

By comparison, she began to feel the Catholic version of Christianity was too distant from Christ himself. Raised Catholic, she was taught that church was an obligation, that not going was a sin, but those were the reasons church was important, not because she felt closer to Jesus or grew from the experience. "In our Catholic church we'd have the gospel reading and an epistle in the New Testament and an Old Testament reading ... but it was kind of repetitive, and we often read the same scriptures year after year." It bothered her that there were many parts of the Bible that they never read. She felt she had a general teaching, but she wanted something more personal, and she wanted to study the Bible on her own, like her brother did. Her Catholic church of the 1970s never held Bible study groups, at least she doesn't recall any.

But she waited to make a change, continued to attend the Catholic Church. "Part of the reason is the guy I was dating and eventually married would barely go to church, and I knew that if I went in the direction my brother did, there was a real possibility I would have lost Bill. So I put that on the back burner, but God kept tugging at my heart," Tricia says.

Her first step down the new path, a path that eventually would, as she feared, create a crisis in her marriage, came when she asked her supervisor at the hospital, a woman she was close with in a working relationship way, if she could attend the supervisor's Bible study group, just check it out once. The once turned into a regular thing, and the two women ended up carpooling to the weekly meeting. They took turns driving, and at night's end, they'd sit parked in the driveway sharing long talks about the night's teachings or just life in general. In summer, they'd roll down the windows and hear the crickets. In winter, they'd turn the car off to not waste gas, and the cold would settle in, and they'd talk until the windows would steam a foggy curtain against the night.

The Mosers ended up living in Indian Village for just a couple of years. Bill was an architect after all, and he naturally wanted a house of his own to work on and shape in his own way. Also, as romantic as Indian Village was, the nearness of Detroit's crime started to play on the couple's minds. A woman was raped a couple of blocks away. There had been some break-ins. They found a duplex to buy in a part of Grosse Pointe Park called the cabbage patch, just a couple of blocks from the

Detroit city border. The communities of Grosse Pointe are known as bastions of wealthy Detroiters, but the cabbage patch is more of an everyman's area. The duplex was maybe 1,500 square feet with a ground-floor apartment where the previous owner continued to live and a second-story apartment where the Mosers lived. Bill could walk down to the corner, hop a bus and ride in along Jefferson Avenue right to work.

The couple set to work on their home. Bill created designs, color schemes. His mom worked at a tile store that a former neighbor from Livonia owned, and Bill bought nice tile at a discount. By outward appearances, it seemed the project brought the couple closer together in that shared mission, working kind of way, but in reality, that togetherness in home renovation masked the fact that Bill and Tricia were moving further apart as they followed divergent lights.

Despite her fears about what it would mean to her marriage, Tricia decided to leave the Catholic Church and pursue her newfound faith as a born-again Christian. Bill's reaction was as she had anticipated. Looking back on it, Bill says, "I was not too happy about that. Even to the point where I felt I was sold a bill of goods. I did not want a Christian wife, or at least not one who was so committed." Maybe going to church on Sunday was okay, and maybe even a Tuesday Bible study, but living and breathing Christianity every moment, day in, day out? Bill had not signed on for that. Bill admits that he began to question whether the marriage could even work if he and his wife were so far apart in such an important part of life.

During this time too, Bill's career continued to evolve. He left the Detroit firm and took a job with a high-profile firm in Birmingham, Michigan, one of Detroit's most elite suburbs. "It was really the best job I could have hoped for at the time," Bill says. The firm he had been working for in Detroit had interesting projects, but the firm in Birmingham had strong connections to the University of Michigan and to major developers in the metro area. As Michigan came out of the recession in the early '80s, Detroit continued to struggle, but a boom ignited in the suburbs. Developers needed architects to design spec office buildings, and Bill's new job was with a firm that specialized in that.

But not long after he started, his sense of discontent returned. "In a job like that, even though you are designing and you have responsibilities, you have a lot of mundane draftsman-type work, and it was a frustrating time of not moving along professionally fast enough." He concedes that he was perhaps realizing his own inadequacies—maybe he had been thinking he could do more architecturally than his talents would allow. Or maybe he was coming to fully understand the commitment it would take to reach where he wanted to be professionally, and he questioned whether success would be worth the price. He contemplated going off on his own. But common doubts plagued him. Would he have the confidence to pull it off? Did he really have the connections he'd need? So he stayed on.

Looking back on it, Bill suspects his dissatisfaction had become evident at work and that some of the partners might have wanted to fire him. A firm partner whom Bill respected suggested Bill take a week off. "Figure out what you want to do," the partner said.

"I recognized that he was going to bat for me," Bill says. He took the week off, reevaluated the job and his attitude, and committed to sticking it out. Keeping a positive attitude "was a daily battle," Bill says. But he felt he was doing okay, though he still had occasional struggles with one junior partner in particular. For a long time Bill had been able to avoid direct contact with the man, but then Bill was assigned to work directly under him on a long-term project. Eventually that assignment and his relationship with the junior partner became a key test in Bill's journey down his path of faith.

Meanwhile, Tricia continued along with her Bible study group. One moment that stays with her all these years later was when another woman in the study group asked the discussion leader about a situation in her marriage that was a lot like Tricia's. The woman was much further down the spiritual path than her husband, and her husband showed little interest in following her. The woman asked the leader what she should do. To Tricia's surprise, the leader said if the man was not going to commit to Christianity and move forward, then the woman should quit the Bible study. "And that's what ended up happening," Tricia says.

But Tricia did not want to quit the Bible study, and eventually the group examined a passage from Peter, 3:1-6, that spoke directly to women with nonbelieving husbands.

From the New International Version of the Bible, the passage goes like this:

1 Wives, in the same way submit yourselves to your own husbands so that, if any of them do not believe the word, they may be won over without words by the behavior of their wives, 2 when they see the purity and reverence of your lives. 3 Your beauty should not come from outward adornment, such as elaborate hairstyles and the wearing of gold jewelry or fine clothes. 4 Rather, it should be that of your inner self, the unfading beauty of a gentle and quiet spirit, which is of great worth in God's sight. 5 For this is the way the holy women of the past who put their hope in God used to adorn themselves. They submitted themselves to their own husbands, 6 like Sarah, who obeyed Abraham and called him her lord. You are her daughters if you do what is right and do not give way to fear.

"That was a huge big wow for me," Tricia says. "Here's how I have to be to be the wife I need to be for the husband that I have. It just gave me direction," she says. She felt it meant that she had to honor her husband and respect his choices and eventually he might join her. She had said those kinds of things in her wedding vows—about respecting and honoring her husband—but more with a sense of ritualism. "The reality of doing it is a different thing," she says. For Tricia, the passage clarified that, despite her husband's unbelieving ways, he remained her leader in the eyes of God, though she could persuade him in subtle ways. "I would honor and respect him with my attitudes," she says. Some of the other ideas that the passage touches upon, "the stuff about outward adorning ... didn't strike me then, but it did later as I grew in my Christian faith."

As I was beginning to write this book about Bill and Tricia, after a year of interviews and having written a couple of chapters, my wife came to me with an old letter from Bill she'd found in the bottom of a filing cabinet drawer. Oddly, there were no other personal letters in the drawer; it was all insurance forms and social security info and bank records and appliance manuals. Bill wrote the letter on November 14, 1983, and I was so struck because, in about a thousand words, it sets a remarkable portrayal of where he was professionally, intellectually and emotionally at the time: a smart, cocky, twenty-five-year-old talking down his bosses and trying to out-intellectualize the intellectuals—the New Yorker editors just not up to his standards. Bill asked me to redact words and phrases that would offend people in the community of faith where his family now lives, but the essence of the letter comes through.

Dear Jeff:

We have an aversion, I think, to buying writing paper in this household. Don't ask me why, but for some reason we just cannot bring ourselves to buy a pad of writing paper. I must have been thinking this very thought when, at work, I got the urge to pilfer the supply cabinet and stock up on some of the firm's legal (letter) pads. Oh well, I guess I can justify this white-collar (slightly yellowed) thievery by assuming that whatever I'm writing to you will have more "worth" than whatever is written in that joint.

It (the eternal 'It') has been a very strange couple of weeks, which have in turn put me in a very strange mood (I'm still not comfortable with funk)—or is it my funky mood which has made these last couple of weeks seem strange? Whatever. I was just sitting here this evening ▮▮▮▮▮▮▮▮▮▮▮▮ *and listening to the Clash ['80s pop-punk band] and reading the best story I've ever read in the New Yorker (almost the only good one) when I realized how similar it was to a really good letter, so I thought that if I longed for a good letter, I'd better get off my butt and write what I'd hope to be a credible one in order to receive one in return. Isn't it strange how bad stories are common but bad letters are so rare? We really should write more! …* ▮▮ *Ma Bell [Michigan's phone monopoly at the time].*

Well, my eyes finally opened to the situation at my place of employment. I guess I had seen it ever since I had started there, but was just [so] glad to be doing 'architecture' that I did not care about what was ahead. By now you're getting the impression that I'm not too happy there. Which is true, for now, but I don't know if I can communicate the problem easily enough. Basically it comes down to the realization that this firm will be, for a long while, a planning / feasibility study–oriented firm, which is fine if you're into marketing and nos. But not fine if you want to design buildings. ▮▮▮▮▮▮▮▮▮▮▮▮▮▮▮▮▮▮▮▮▮▮

It really is a longer story than that, but it's not worth any more ink. I've had a couple of interviews and am trying to line up more—so we'll see what happens.

Back to the New Yorker story. When I get the N.Y. I usually turn to the stories and look to see if any are four pages or shorter, and if there are I usually read them, unless it's an Updike story, in which case I immediately curse at all the gods and take the magazine into the john and throw it on the floor, where it is sure to get ▮▮ *dribbled on it and eventually thousands of hairs sticking to it from my ever-receding hairline* ▮▮▮▮▮▮▮▮▮▮▮▮ *But finally, after nine months, they finally printed a GOOD story that never seemed to end. I'll save you this issue, or at least that story. I'm so sick of the New Yorker and its editor's political/editorial drivel that I could puke. It has gotten to the point where I only read the odd story. Most poems are junk—and look for the even rarer ad* ▮▮▮▮▮▮▮▮▮▮▮▮▮▮▮▮▮▮▮▮▮▮

The story I like is Edisto, by Padgett Powell. Warlock [Jim Harrison novel] was very, very GOOD. It rang truer than any book I've read, I think. It was simply a good book as Edisto was simply a good story. I could intellectualize them, but what purpose does that serve? I think 'good' should become an adjective again w/out having to define what the ▮▮ *it is. Good is good. Junk is junk.*

So Jeff, how have you been? Sorry for this monologue—I only mean half of what I say, but monologues are fun—once in a while. As I was saying before, I was reading Edisto and thinking what a good story it was and hoping it would never end when I thought how much it was like reading a good letter and how well you write—we really are ▮▮▮ for not writing more often. I mean, we communicate often, but we really do not write often enough—letters are good stories. Don't think for a minute that the previously mentioned wine has reduced me to sentimentality—it hasn't. Even if it did, which it probably has to some degree, so what. Everyone who has ever written about the evils of sentimentality have been the biggest sentimental ▮▮▮ on the Earth. Hemingway was the worst. Harrison not far behind.

Anyone who doesn't see and feel life has no life—you can only be so detached. If you are utterly detached you're worthless. What is worthless and to whom?

Every time we visit you our longing for the area in which you live grows more intense. It is one of the few places I've been that I would want to spend a great deal of time at. To me it has a sense of place—which is rare especially, in my eyes. This is said not to discourage you from moving to other regions. Edisto was set in the Carolinas. But I'm sure no other place will give you the feeling that Leelanau does.

Well, time to wrap this monologue up. Hope it isn't too boring. Bruce & Amy [Bill's oldest brother and his wife] have a baby—Catrina Marie (cool name) sounds Serbian-Russian.

We are going to the cottage this coming weekend. Look forward to that.

Also looking forward to X-country skiing up at your place & going to new wave bars down here w/ you two—let's do them both this winter.

Have been fairly 'gone' dance-wise, at the last parties we've been too—'gone' in that the people watching me would probably sum up my condition as saying, "he's gone." Which is a good way to be right now.

Give Linda my love Tricia sends hers. Bill.

Conditions under which this letter was written: Wine, slight depression. Music: Waters, Clash, Police, Bowie, Doors. (The usual stuff of life.)

What Bill couldn't have known as he penned the letter is that the biggest transformation in his life, one that would completely alter his heretofore chosen life path, was about to happen.

A New
Path

When the Mosers' first son was born in 1987, they named him Tristan. It's a beautiful name, but in some ways the choice illustrated something of the divide the Mosers straddled at the time. The name Tristan was inspired by the lead character of the Jim Harrison novella *Legends of the Fall*, a character later played by Brad Pitt in the film adaptation. In the story, Tristan is a spirited, defiant, hard-drinking and irreverent Montana rancher, scorner of ritual and ceremony and a full-on embracer of the wild parts of an earthly existence. In one vivid scene, when Tristan learns his younger brother had been killed in World War I, Tristan sneaks away from his own regiment, secretly finds his brother's body and cuts out his heart so it can be buried back on the Montana ranch. If the Tristan character had any religion at all, it was a vague adaptation of Native American belief. At the time, Bill was a big fan of Harrison, and the name seemed to express much of who Bill was, but I wondered how the name settled with Tricia, who was becoming more convicted in her faith.

Thinking back on that time of life, Bill says, "I abhorred the thought of a Christian lifestyle, or what I thought was a Christian lifestyle. I felt I didn't know any Christians who were really genuine, people who were really doing what they talked about."

But all the while, Tricia continued to go to Bible study, and she had by now left the Catholic church. Bill concedes that despite his general reservations about Christians, he was especially impressed by one of the families whom Tricia met through Bible study. The man was an auto executive, high on the Ford org chart, and the family had four daughters, some of them teenagers who babysat Tristan on occasion. "The daughters were kind of amazing, very bright, and Tricia and I were attracted to the family," Bill says. "But they home-schooled their children, which we thought was kind of strange, but we were curious about it at the same time." It was the latter half of the 1980s, home-schooling had just ignited in America, and most people viewed it as something for people on the fringe.

The couple from Bible study invited Tricia and Bill over for dinner one night. Even though Bill genuinely liked and respected the family, mostly he agreed to go because the family lived in a house designed by an architect that Bill had studied, and he wanted to see it up close. What Bill didn't know is the couple also had an agenda that night. They wanted to convince Bill to go with Tricia to a weeklong conference about Christian family life at Cobo Hall, a 13,000-seat arena where the Detroit Pistons basketball team played at the time. The Christian conference would happen every night after work and then culminate with two all-day sessions on Friday and Saturday.

Tricia had attended the conference twice in previous years, but Bill had always declined. And this year, he had no intention of committing to a weeklong Christian conference either. He didn't want to go for even one night. "But I was too much of a man-pleaser to say I didn't want to go," he says. When the friends encouraged Bill to go, he said yes.

And Bill lived up to his word. He went, figuring it would be a one-night event for him, and on a Monday night, he and Tricia settled into their seats in Cobo Hall. To Bill's surprise, the main speaker wasn't even in attendance; he was on a gigantic screen. "He was this neatly dressed, prim and proper man in his fifties with carefully parted short hair. He was neat as a pin, the personification of the kind of Christian man that I loathed," Bill says. "I thought, This guy has nothing to tell me. He was so stereotypical of what I thought of as a Christian man."

Bill casually listened as the speaker started working through his material, and then the man said something that changed Bill's life. He said, "You must put off the old man and put on the new man; put off the old life and put on the new life." And for whatever reason, this line—which Bill thinks he must have heard several times before during various Bible studies—struck him with an electrifying jolt of clarity. Bill calls the phenomena, that instant inspiration, "divine spark." He says that this is the moment when Jesus truly came into his heart, when Bill's religious experience transformed from being a "head" thing, an intellectual exercise in ritual and religiosity, to something that let him live a fully formed spiritual life. "I had planned to go one night, but after that I couldn't stay away," he says. He went with Tricia to the entire conference, every night after work that week, all day Friday, all day Saturday.

As odd as it might sound, Bill didn't tell Tricia at the time about his experience with the divine spark. He doesn't really know why, doesn't have an explanation. "Back then I just wasn't the kind of person to communicate those things. I'm sure Tricia sensed a difference, but I can't really say for sure." If nothing else, she would have figured something was different just based on the fact that Bill was willing to go to the rest of the seminar and not bail out after the first night.

Tricia confirms that Bill didn't openly discuss the divine spark moment until a long time afterward. "It might have even been a couple of years before I fully understood the importance of what happened then," she says. As Bill suspected, Tricia did see a difference in him, in his desire to read the Bible, in his desire to share thoughts about what he'd read.

But despite subtle changes on the outside, inside himself, Bill says the divine spark led to immediate and dramatic changes in all aspects of his life—at work, at home and at church—changes that only increased the more he pursued his faith.

He recalls the most noticeable changes happening at work that very week. "It transformed my whole outlook," he says. Between the faith conference and the divine spark, Bill felt he could see new truth in the Bible and, importantly, how the Bible's teachings had relevance in daily life, how Jesus's teachings could actually make a difference. A main and immediate change was that Bill came to acknowledge that he had a problem with authority figures.

Bill found guidance in scripture that addressed that very thing, the role of authority in life. "Jesus would teach that in everyday life, you can't serve two masters. You will love the one and hate the other, hold to one and reject the other," Bill says. He developed a new perspective for who he was at work, what his role was. "I understood I had to stop trying to promote myself and my abilities, and I was there to serve who had hired me. I was more respectful, and that ultimately did show up with the junior partner."

Bill and the junior partner had never hit it off. And Bill felt fortunate that he had little interaction with the man. But the junior partner was assigned to run an entire project, and Bill was put on the team under the man's authority. "This was God's test for me, and I was failing at it miserably," Bill says. "I felt he was going about things the wrong way, and I just chafed under him."

Bill felt himself returning to the daily battle of keeping his attitude up. "The guy was autocratic and totally not artistic, a plodding thinker and not a designer, though he was in charge of design," Bill says. A key point of conflict arose when the junior partner instructed Bill on how to set up the drawing package for the building project. Bill knew "clear as day" that the senior partner who was ultimately in charge of the project wanted it done differently, and Bill said so. But the junior partner pulled rank and told Bill not to argue. After Bill had put a lot of time into the drawing package, the senior partner came around to inspect. "He got visibly upset when he stopped at my desk," Bill says. The senior partner called the junior partner over and asked why he told Bill to do the work that way, and the junior partner denied he'd given that instruction.

Bill got hot and spoke his mind, but the senior partner believed the junior partner, told Bill to redo the work and the two men left him sitting at his desk fuming. Bill remembered the phrase that changed his life. Put off the old man and put on the new man. "It was clear as day that God was saying, 'You are not going anywhere until you are under that man's authority and are the servant you need to be.'" But Bill felt too that he had to submit to God as well. "I said, if this is your will, you will have to give me the strength to do it, because I cannot do it by myself."

Bill worked on the project. "I gave up in my heart and God gave me the strength," he says. He stayed on the project to completion and then started another one under the junior partner. Bill stayed agreeable, and the relationship was not a struggle. One time, when the second project was well underway, Bill was talking with the junior partner and the man told Bill it had been a pleasure working with him. Bill knew then that he had risen to God's challenge, passed the test, and Bill then felt free to move on with his life and begin his own design construction business.

At a time of crisis and consternation, Tricia listened to the Bible and submitted to her husband. At a time of conflict and anger, Bill listened to the Bible and submitted to his boss. Submission occupies an odd place in America today. If there is a unifying theme to the narrative that media presents, it is that America's heroes do not submit, and the natural extension of that idea is that if we have courage and honor and character, we do not submit either.

Weak people submit. Strong people do not submit. But of course, that is a cartoon idea, a fallacy. The most courageous fighter in the Marines knows that submission to the line of authority is one of the most essential pillars on which the military stands. The media presents the late corporate icon Steve Jobs, Apple computer CEO, as a rebel who submitted to nobody, but Apple's 80,000 employees submit every single day. But of course, the media only tells us about Steve Jobs.

In daily practice we all submit, but submission is something we are taught to deny or at least to pretend we don't do. And that's perhaps why we from general society would naturally become uncomfortable when Tricia and Bill talk openly about a plain interpretation of the Bible's directive to submit to a line of authority.

For Bill and Tricia, the notion of submitting is central to their belief and grows largely from what is called "the headship order," from the King James Bible:

1 Corinthians 11:3 - But I would have you know, that the head of every man is Christ; and the head of the woman [is] the man; and the head of Christ [is] God. [King James Bible]

In Bill's mind, the notion of headship has been distorted and wrongly wielded by people who want to exploit or dominate, and especially by men who want to dominate women. "That has been abused and so now that is not an attractive idea. But there are safeguards in the Bible, and when the headship principles are abused, the man is ignoring Christ's other teachings." Elsewhere in the Bible, Jesus tells each husband he should be willing to lay down his life for his wife, just as Christ did for his church. A man who follows that teaching and is truly willing to lay down his life for his wife would never abuse his wife physically or emotionally, Bill says.

Breaking
Away

About the time Bill had resolved his relationship with the junior partner at work, Bill was also doing a freelance job designing a large addition to a house in Grosse Pointe. The owner was a wealthy businessman who didn't trust anybody other than Bill to build the job precisely as Bill had designed it. The client asked Bill to be general contractor on the job, overseeing every detail of construction and managing all the tradespeople. Bill saw it as a door opening to the next dream job, and he resigned from the Birmingham architecture firm to go independent as a design/build firm.

The project was a stately 1920s Tudor home, with classic details like intricate oak trim. Bill designed an addition that grew off the back and rose two stories. The design expanded the kitchen, added a breakfast nook, a family room, another bedroom upstairs. The project was nearly equivalent in scope to building a moderate-sized house. Again Bill had the feeling that he was fulfilling a dream. Not that being an independent Christian businessman was easy. Bill concedes there were many stressful times. "Being new in business and trying to be honest and do everything right, it was a challenge, and when you'd come across people that took advantage of that—" his voice trails off. "And I made my own number of mistakes."

By now, Bill and Tricia were in their mid-thirties and they had four children: Tristan, Timothy, Aaron and Sarah. The couple decided Tricia should quit working to be home with the children, which eased the stress of managing their home, but added financial pressure to Bill's business.

By now, too, Tristan and Timothy were getting close to kindergarten age, and Bill and Tricia were having reservations about the curriculum in public schools. "It wasn't the academics," Bill says. "Grosse Pointe has some of the best schools in the country." But the Mosers were worried about what they perceived as a vague antagonism toward teaching Christian principles.

The Mosers were concerned about a lack of "or even hostility toward any kind of Christian or faith-based learning in public schools," Bill says.

The Mosers also wanted character training to be an integral part of their children's education, and they saw little of that in public schools.

The solution they arrived at—home schooling, a practice they'd viewed as being "kind of strange" just a few years prior—became a momentous development in their journey of faith.

They bought textbooks from a Mennonite publishing house, and to counter the isolation that can accompany home schooling, the Mosers connected with other home-schoolers around Detroit for weekly playtimes. They met like-minded families for playtime at parks. They regularly rented a roller skating rink together, swapping in family-oriented music on the sound system. They shared ideas and support. Home schooling achieved many of the things Bill and Tricia had hoped it would, and most important, it furthered their vision of life with a close-knit family that was intentional about togetherness. And with control over the curriculum, Bill and Tricia were able to bring in the character education they wanted. The textbooks, for example, told stories based on the animal kingdom that would celebrate or criticize character traits, like, say, a beaver story would celebrate diligence and hard work. Some other animal would reveal why laziness is bad.

But home schooling also opened the Mosers' eyes to something they hadn't anticipated. Home-schoolers, despite being spread out among Detroit's far-flung suburbs and coming from an assortment of Christian denominations, had built a remarkably strong sense of community, and it laid the foundations for Bill and Tricia coming to see community of faith as something bigger and more integral to their day. Far more than a reassuring nicety or a thing of comfort, community of faith became an essential component of a fully realized spiritual life.

"In the home-schooling group I saw how I felt church should be working—more interactive, more part of our daily lives, more accountability because there was a standard we wanted to maintain in education and morally because it was faith based," Bill says. By teaching their children in their home every day, the practice of their faith became much more a moment-to-moment part of life than a "Sunday service, Wednesday Bible study" kind of experience. Sharing faith in a stronger community way made the personal experience with God richer.

As Christian denominations across America place ever-greater emphasis on the individual's relationship with Jesus, Bill believes they need to keep in mind Jesus's broader teachings about the importance of community and church. "It's true that faith, first of all, is a coming of the individual to God," Bill says. "But Jesus established the church, and he called his church his own body and said that we are parts of the body, and each member is like a finger or an eye or arm, and the foot can't say to the hand that I have no need of you." Not that a sense of brotherhood was absent in their regular church—the Mosers felt they belonged to a good church and there were clear and strong examples of community—but the home-schooling experience made the Mosers realize that a sense of religious community and brotherhood could be woven more deeply into their daily lives. That desire to be a part of a very close-knit community of faith came to shape their lives and their next move, because, after all, despite the sense of community that the home-schoolers provided, they did not comprise a church, and the Mosers knew they wanted to be a part of a church.

At this point in their lives, Bill and Tricia were coming to see with greater clarity the key elements that would guide them through the dramatic life changes in the years ahead, though they had no idea just how dramatic those changes would be. They knew they wanted faith at the center of their lives in a moment-by-moment, day-in-day-out way. Equally, they wanted to be part of a community that shared their view of faith. They wanted to spend days together as a family and stay focused on the relationships with their children, and those relationships would be guided by the Bible. They knew that they wanted to make a living in a way that did not pull them physically apart from their family and children and home.

Also at this time they began to feel more distant from the church they'd been attending for more than a decade. "We were in the routine for thirteen years," Bill says, looking back on their days in Grosse Pointe. "We went to a Protestant church, we worked with the youth group, our children went there," he says. But after a change in pastors, the church changed. The new pastors seemed overly interested in growing the membership and in defining the way parishioners related to Jesus.

"More and more I questioned, Why don't we just do what Jesus says?" Bill says. In other words, take the Bible at face value, a plain interpretation that would guide daily life.

Then on one Sunday during the Gulf War of the early 1990s, something happened that elevated their concerns. During the regular church service, a military color guard marched in formation up the center aisle of the church. They took position at the front of the church, and people sang patriotic songs.

"It was very troubling," Tricia says. "We talked about it in the car on the way home." Tricia proclaims a love for her country, but her religious beliefs guide her here. "What really bothered me is that my Christian nephew could be called up to go to another country and kill another Christian, or worse, kill a non-Christian who won't go to heaven."

Bill recalls sitting in the pew, watching the event unfold and thinking, Does this please God? It is so nationalistic. What does it have to do with Jesus Christ? "It felt like we were glorifying our nation's power and might at the expense of God-created beings, which seemed so contrary to His teaching, that in our weakness He will make us strong," Bill says. He wondered if he was the only one feeling that way. Bill was so perplexed by his own reaction, he asked God why He was even bringing these thoughts to him. Jesus teaches that when in doubt, turn to scripture, and that's where Bill looked for answers.

Bill views the event as another turning point in his evolution of faith because his thoughts, his reaction, his research in the Bible, were all independent of any outside influencers other than "God's word and His spirit." The topic had not come up in conversation during a Bible study, nor with anybody else. He never even brought up the issue to anybody in church because he felt it was so outside the commonly held belief there. He concedes, "I had been in full support of the war not that long ago and would have felt that way myself."

Bill and Tricia felt the church was going in a new direction, and they felt they'd take the opportunity to go in a new direction of their own. One Sunday they didn't go to the church, and they never went again. Thirteen years of churchgoing and sharing of faith and now it was time to move on.

The Thumb
Years

By now the couple had determined that living in the country could bring them closer to their life vision, and they decided to move to a farming area about ninety miles north of Detroit in a region called Michigan's Thumb (on the map the region looks like the thumb of a mitten). "I had a vision of farming, having a house and a big garden and saw how those experiences could be learning experiences for my children outside the classroom and books, more hands-on learning," Bill says.

They bought sixteen acres on a land contract and committed to building the house debt-free, buying construction materials a little at a time as they could afford. Their search to find affordable lumber led to their first encounters with the Amish.

Bill designed the family house and for lumber approached an Amish man who ran a sawmill in Gladwin, near the cottage the Moser family had owned since the 1950s. Bill had been vaguely curious about the Amish for some time, ever since he saw them moving to the Gladwin countryside in the late 1970s. "I saw fallow land being farmed again, decrepit farmhouses being fixed up," he says. "And I noticed that the people made do with what they had."

One time Bill was canoeing down a narrow river near Gladwin, and a massive Belgian draft horse crashed out of the shoreline thicket. From Bill's low vantage point in the canoe, the horse looked huge, majestic and beautiful as it splashed across the river directly in front of him, and then disappeared on the other side. The horse was an Amish workhorse, and looking back on the moment—the tight quarters of the river, the water, the tremendous, muscular presence of the horse careening by, then vanishing—it's tempting to think of the event as a foreshadowing of the force that the Amish would play in Bill and Tricia's lives.

The Amish sawmill owner, Joni Mast (pronounced JOE-nigh), was a lifelong Amish, friendly and curious about the Mosers and their Christian beliefs. There was something about Joni Mast's life that made a big impression on the Mosers. They saw that the man's children were with the parents throughout the day. The family did not have the ten- or twelve-hour daily separation between children and parents that many American families accept as a part of 21st-century existence—babies dropped off at daycare at 6:30 a.m. and picked up at 6:30 p.m.

"I'd been thinking for a long time that I wanted to shrink my world, create a life where work, recreation, family and religion were all one, a whole, not so fragmented," Bill says. He went home and—this in the days before the Internet—sat in a chair in his living room and looked up Amish in the encyclopedia his dad and mom had bought when he was a child. He learned that the Amish were part of the Anabaptist Reformation and had been around since the 1600s.

Bill's and Tricia's curiosity kept drawing them closer to the Amish as the months went by, and eventually the couple hired Amish builders to frame their home in the Thumb. Sometimes Bill would drive the crew to and from the job site. He'd listen to them talk in their dialect of Pennsylvania German, curious about what they were saying, but, he concedes, he really didn't converse directly with them all that much, so his understanding of the faith remained vague.

With the desire to push further down the path of faith and family, Bill dissolved his construction company and took a job as a construction manager for a small developer. The job offered him more flexibility and removed the constant pressure of keeping cash flowing in his business, especially with Tricia not working. And when the Amish builders had the home roughed in and sealed against the elements, the Mosers moved to their new home in the Thumb, near a tiny town called Memphis.

Bill and Tricia both have extremely fond memories of their time near Memphis "It was kind of a 'best of times' for us," Bill recalls. They had sixteen acres on a quiet country road, and a short walk to the north took them to the bank of a little river called the Belle River. Memphis felt so right-sized too for the family's new life vision: just a grocery store, hardware store, gas station and ice cream shop and the donut shop that sold donuts for 25 cents apiece. The family planted its first big garden and bought chickens.

The children loved all that space and the country life. The Mosers continued to home school.

"We really felt we'd broken away from general society. We felt we had a say in our lives," Bill says. The fact that Bill and Tricia loved their transition so much in some ways seems like the obvious outcome to fulfilling a life vision: of course they'd be happy there. But more broadly, the move also brought the first dramatic scaling back in the technology of their lives and what people in general society would view as a significant downgrade in standard of living. It says a great deal about their changed life emphasis that they recall these days as a best of times thing.

The Amish carpenters had finished their work, but to call the home finished would have been a large overstatement. In many communities in America, the Mosers would never have qualified for an occupancy permit. For starters, there was no electricity run to the home. The choice was not one based on religious considerations; it cost too much to run the wire in from the nearest connection, and the couple was still determined to build the house debt-free. Bill hooked up a generator to run a couple of small things, but otherwise, the family lighted their home with kerosene lamps, had no clothes washer or dryer and no television.

The kitchen was not installed when they moved in, and Bill never completed it during the year and a half the Mosers lived there. They washed dishes in a laundry washtub. For beds, the two oldest boys slept on a futon that lay across a stack of boards that were to be used for finishing the home interior—in the space where the kitchen was supposed to be. Aaron, the third-oldest son, slept on a mattress laid atop another stack of wood. Sarah slept on a crib mattress in the living room, and Matthew, the fifth child, slept in a porta-crib. Bill and Tricia slept in the room where the family held school, which they called the schoolroom. It was a far cry from their days living among the leafy boulevards of Indian Village, rolling in their BMW past manors built by kings of American industry.

With their happiness now based on time with family and faith, Tricia viewed the situation like this: "We enjoyed it while we had it," Tricia says. "It was a little rustic, not the modern conveniences, like we didn't have electricity for quite a while, but we just weren't in a hurry to get it."

Tricia's sister's husband, an accountant, couldn't bear the thought of a house built without electricity, in part because he figured the house would have no resale value, so he offered to pay for the electrical installation. The Mosers eventually accepted the offer, based on his reasoning, not because they longed for electricity. Eventually the Mosers paid him back.

At one point, Tricia's longtime best friend during school and college connected with her and came out to visit. The two had sung in school choirs together, and were raised in church-going families—though her friend had attended a different denomination. They quizzed each other late into the night for anatomy tests at Wayne State University. They'd double-dated with their future husbands for years. Throughout so many of the important coming-of-age years and moments, "We were connected at the hip," Tricia says. Tricia showed her friend the chickens, the garden, the beautiful land that stretched all around, the home-school teaching room, but also, of course, the unfinished house, the lack of a kitchen, the children's beds on stacks of wood, the absence of electricity. They talked about life's changes, and Tricia explained the journey of faith and family she and Bill had followed. After that visit, they drifted apart and have not spoken in decades.

Meanwhile, the Mosers' search for the ideal church community continued to evolve. They sought out the most conservative Baptist church they could find near their home in the Thumb.

By now, Tricia had begun to follow a more literal interpretation of the Bible's instruction on how women should dress, and she had begun to wear a veil as a head covering. She was surprised, then, when she went to the little country church and saw a woman wearing a derby-style hat. Tricia suspected the woman—who was about Tricia's age—wore the derby because of scriptural dictates, and the woman told her that that was indeed the case. "She didn't know how else to do it," Tricia says. "She was believing and practicing it the best she could, but she was on her own, because the church did not support the idea of head covering." Tricia shared her veil pattern with the woman so she could sew her own.

Tricia learned another woman at the church also wore a head covering when, not long after they started attending the church, Bill and Tricia visited her and her husband at their home. They were surprised to see the wife was wearing a head covering in her house—they had not seen her wear it in church. The woman explained that there had been a disruption over the idea of head coverings in the church, and her husband asked her to not wear it there because it offended some people, so she wore the head covering only at home. "But she wanted to wear it so badly because she believed in it," Tricia says. When she saw Tricia's veil, the woman felt she'd met a kindred spirit and wanted to discuss scripture and head coverings. "It was kind of ironic that I ended up going to a church where some of the people believed like I did," Tricia says.

Tricia describes her evolution of faith as slow and gradual, and her evolution to wearing a head covering is a surprisingly important part of that evolution. Reflecting on the "outward adornment" piece of Peter, 3:1-6, Tricia proceeded along the arc of simplifying her fashion step by step. She first stopped wearing makeup, but still wore a little blush. She then stopped wearing blush. She stopped wearing jewelry. She continued to cut her bangs. "But then I got convicted and stopped cutting my hair," she says. No more "jazzy haircuts," she says. Her hair is now long, but she wears it tied up. "Scripture says my hair is my glory, for my husband's pleasure only," she says. When Tricia was pregnant with Sarah, she began wearing long dresses—pants and shorts stayed in the closet. A couple of years later, when Matthew was about one, she started wearing a head covering. She came to believe the Bible says you should pray unceasingly. "So I began to wear it all the time," Tricia says. She figures her fashion transformation was a three-year journey.

Tricia knew a woman who made the transition to plain dress and head covering overnight. She was a professional, a counselor in a social services agency, and one day she abandoned her old wardrobe and showed up at work dressed in the new way. "I was either too dense or not brave enough to do that," Tricia says.

Even in Tricia's family, a family of strong Christians, the head covering is not discussed much. "We don't quarrel about it or push a point. It's just something we believe we should do, and we want to be with people who want to do that same thing," Bill says. Beyond what the head covering means for personal religious fulfillment, the head covering is a central and visible element that helps create that sense of community in faith that the Mosers so deeply sought. The head covering draws people together. "Most Christians who believe in head covering have a strong sense that Christians should be in a community, submitting to one another, being accountable to one another," Bill says. "So it is a big thing."

As much as Bill and Tricia loved their new place in Memphis, Michigan, and enjoyed the little Baptist church, they still felt they had not yet found that element of Christian community they'd come to see as essential to having a fulfilled spiritual life. The issue of head covering—supported by a few, but opposed by most people in the church they attended—was a daily and visible reminder that they'd not quite found what they were seeking.

By now, too, they had visited the Amish church in Manton and felt they'd witnessed the kind of fully immersed community of faith they had imagined. In most churches in America people gather for Sunday service and in somewhat scripted ways—meetings to discuss topics, or issues or Bible study. "Your involvement is programmed around certain things instead of the simple fact of being a community," Bill says. To him, it wasn't a natural way to bond with fellow believers. "Even if you go to church with people, it is hard to get to know them if that is the only way you are interacting. It just didn't seem like what Christ wanted for his church," Bill says.

Bill and Tricia wanted to be in a community that more closely shared their views of scripture, and the issue of a head covering or not became one more thing that pulled them toward the Amish. They had begun talking with Tom Kuhn and his family, who had crossed over from general society to Amish. They began visiting Amish families. They researched the faith.

And just as longtime relationships were strained and even broken as the Mosers moved along the evolution in their faith, new relationships opened up in the Amish community. The Mosers' new friends, the Kuhns, had transitioned from general society to the Amish life and had moved to Manton, a small farming community a couple hours' drive from the Mosers. The Mosers began to visit the community and another one nearby called Ovid, where they would eventually move.

Tricia, recalling the thoughts swirling in her mind at the time, says, "Sometimes we'd go visit and I couldn't even believe we were visiting there. I'd think, We can't do this. How can we do this? And then I'd meet them and I'd look at their lifestyle, and I'd start thinking, Well, maybe we can do this. I don't know!"

Inspired by
Joni Mast

W hen Bill and Tricia tell their story of transitioning to Amish life, the sawmill owner Joni Mast figures large in the tale. "I tell people he's the one to blame for being so friendly and open," Bill says. "And I needed somebody like that."

Bill and Tricia knew about Joni before they ever met him. They had taken notice when, about the mid-'80s, an Amish family had moved into a house on M-18, a highway they drove to reach the long-time Moser family cottage. The house was little more than a shack at the time, but soon a sawmill opened there. And then the family built a larger traditional Amish house, a spacious and handsome white saltbox. In that evolution, Bill saw the same steady progress toward a goal that he'd been impressed with at other Amish homesteads in the area that had begun to proliferate in the late '70s.

By the time Bill met Joni, he and Tricia were moving toward a more literal interpretation of Christ's teachings. They were living by such principles as nonviolent resistance, beginning to see the value of a strong community of faith that viewed Christ as a moment-by-moment part of the day, had begun to contemplate Tricia wearing a head covering. But the couple was nowhere near to being Amish, and they had no idea that many of the principles of faith they had arrived at nearly on their own were shared by the Amish people. In fact, they still had only the most rudimentary notion of what Amish even meant.

When the Mosers were ready to start buying lumber to build their house in the Thumb, they asked the lumberjack neighbor at their Northern Michigan cottage for advice. He suggested they head to the Amish sawmill Bill and Tricia had passed so many times on their way to the cottage. With their goal of building the house debt-free, they figured they could save a lot of money buying rough-sawn lumber direct from the mill.

"I was all nervous," Bill says of his first meeting with Joni. "I was not sure who these people were, and I was wondering, How does he view me? Does he view me like everybody else who comes through the door?" Bill wore shorts and a T-shirt on that first visit. He had contemplated putting on more modest attire, like long pants, but he reasoned that he didn't want to "be something that I wasn't—that is how I dressed at the time."

Bill left the family at the cottage and drove over in the Chevy Suburban. He brought the long list of lumber he wanted, not just framing materials, but planks for the roof, boards for flooring and the interior walls. "I had all these dreams, and I wondered if he'd just tell me I'm nuts and to go to a regular lumberyard," Bill says.

Joni had set up his office in the small, brick-patterned asphalt-sided building that his family had lived in while they built the sawmill and big house. Bill knocked on the door, and Joni came walking over from the mill. A couple of Joni's young children came with him to meet with Bill in the office. "I remember the kids staring at me, and I remember one of them reaching over and touching me," Bill says.

Bill took it all in. Late afternoon light illuminated the small office, otherwise, there were no lights on. There was a woodstove, some leather belts and harness pieces hanging on the walls. Axes and big circular sawmill blades also hung neatly on the wall. And the man's children were with him throughout the day. Bill noticed they were inquisitive and confident and respectful. And the family house was right there, just across the driveway.

But what Bill remembers most was a potent and vivid feeling: This guy Joni has it made.

"I thought, This is nice. This is what I would want. But it still seemed like this was his life. Could it even be a life for somebody like me?" Bill recalls.

Joni was the first Amish person Bill had ever spoken to. "I didn't even know what kind of religion they were. I suspected they were Christian, but you know, some sub-groups of Mormons still practice polygamy. I wondered does he have more than one wife? Does the community pool their money like I'd heard some Christian communities do, stuff like that." When Bill went home to look up Amish in the encyclopedia, in reading, one thing that stayed with him was learning that it wasn't non-believers who had burned the Amish predecessors at the stake and drowned them in sacks by the hundreds back in the 1500s, it was other Christians— Catholics and Protestants.

Joni asked Bill about the church he attended. "And little did Joni know I was full of my own questions and my own doubts about what I'd been taught about normal Christian life and that God seemed to be working on my heart, that something else is out there."

At the time, Bill did not know that so many of the things he had been seeking, so many of the teachings he'd been wondering about in the Bible, were practiced by the Amish. One thing Joni asked about was head coverings. Bill explained that he and Tricia had studied the passages about head coverings and that Tricia had begun wearing a veil. Later, as Bill met other Amish people, he saw that Amish viewed head coverings as a gauge of how literal people are about following the Bible's teachings. "Do they really believe the Bible, or have they been taught to excuse the teachings of the Bible?" Bill says.

Bill and Joni also shared long scriptural talks about the individual's relationship with Jesus, and Bill was struck by the Amish's starkly different interpretation of the permanence or impermanence of being saved. "Most mainstream Christian churches, evangelical, Protestant, would believe that once you give your life to Christ, you are born again and you are sealed for the rest of your life. Nearly regardless of what you do, you can't fall away," Bill says. But the Amish and Mennonite churches clearly believe you can fall away and be in a lost condition, a condition that would be even worse than if you had never accepted Christ to begin with.

In those conversations with Joni—sometimes an hour long, sometimes a half-hour, sometimes in Joni's office, sometimes outside by Bill's Suburban as they worked together loading a trailer of lumber—Bill would think back to the many years he and Tricia had worked with the youth group at his church. "We'd go to winter camp and have speakers and get the kids all pumped up emotionally and then slam them with the guilt of their sin and convince them to come to Christ. But then they'd go back home, and the emotionalism would wear off, and they'd go back to whatever it was they were doing. We saw a hardness being built into them," Bill says.

Bill concedes he could see both sides of the argument. After all, he had been taught that you could spit in Jesus's face and He would still take you to heaven. And Jesus had said that nobody could snatch you from His hands. Joni agreed, yes, nobody can force you away from Jesus, but you yourself can choose to walk away, and that is a different thing. Joni's reasoning stayed with Bill, and he shared it with Tricia. "Those were the weighty scriptural things we talked about, and I just loved it," Bill recalls.

The conversations with Joni lasted for about a year as Bill and Tricia continued to buy lumber one trailer load at a time as they could afford it. Bill would head over to Joni's, load up the lumber and drive it back to their cottage ten minutes away on Island Lake. Rather than kiln drying the wood, Bill employed a technique call stack and sticker. He stacked the wood with one-inch spacers between each board to allow air to circulate through the stack and dry the boards. He covered the stacks with tin roofing to keep them dry. Eventually the Mosers had more than a dozen large stacks of lumber sitting in the yard behind the cottage, like a visual representation of the spiritual principles of the Amish collecting and gaining weight in Bill and Tricia's minds.

Eventually Bill mustered the courage to ask Joni about his lifestyle, about the way he relates to his family and community and faith. Bill wondered if there was something written up about how they lived. "I didn't really know what I was asking for," Bill says. He only knew that he was seeing a lifestyle, a community, an approach to faith that he had dreamed of at some level, and he knew he needed to know more.

Joni gave him a copy of a document that is foundational for Amish, Mennonites and other Anabaptists. Titled the *Dordrecht Confession of Faith* and commonly called the *18 Articles of Faith*, it was written in 1632 in Dordrecht, Netherlands, by Mennonites wanting to answer critics who charged that Anabaptists were heretics. The document lays out principles of belief related to nonviolent resistance, non-participation in government, shunning and more.

Among the 18 articles, Bill and Tricia read XIV about revenge: "As regards revenge, that is, to oppose an enemy with the sword, we believe and confess that the Lord Christ has forbidden and set aside to His disciples and followers all revenge and retaliation, and commanded them to render to no one evil for evil, or cursing for cursing, but to put the sword into the sheath, or, as the prophets have predicted, to beat the swords into ploughshares."

They read article XVII about shunning: "Concerning the withdrawing from, or shunning the separated, we believe and confess, that if any one, either through his wicked life or perverted doctrine, has so far fallen that he is separated from God, and, consequently, also separated and punished by the church, the same must, according to the doctrine of Christ and His apostles, be shunned, without distinction, by all the fellow members of the church, especially those to whom it is known, in eating, drinking, and other similar intercourse, and no company be had with him that they may not become contaminated by intercourse with him, nor made partakers of his sins; but that the sinner may be made ashamed, pricked in his heart, and convicted in his conscience, unto his reformation."

They read article VII about Baptism: "Concerning baptism we confess that all penitent believers, who, through faith, regeneration, and the renewing of the Holy Ghost, are made one with God, and are written in heaven, must, upon such Scriptural confession of faith, and renewing of life, be baptized with water, in the most worthy name of the Father, and of the Son, and of the Holy Ghost, according to the command of Christ, and the teaching, example, and practice of the apostles, to the burying of their sins, and thus be incorporated into the communion of the saints; henceforth to learn to observe all things which the Son of God has taught, left, and commanded His disciples.

Regarding the *18 Articles of Faith*, Bill says, "It was exactly what I needed. It solidified that these are the Christians that I want to be with." Bill began to feel that somehow, remarkably, he had found people who believed in scripture in so many of the same ways he and Tricia had come to believe.

But while the statement of faith clarified many questions Bill and Tricia had, they were still looking for something that spelled out the rules for Amish living, the boundaries for negotiating daily life. If Bill and Tricia were really going to consider this way, they needed to know a lot more. Where was it set forth that Amish should drive with horses, for example, or not use electricity—what were the boundaries on those things? What about making a living—were there special rules about doing business? Was there a document like that? It turned out there is, sort of. The document is called the Ordnung, and each little Amish church around the world approves its own version, that is, each church can modify the document to fit its particular circumstances. In reality, though, many share the same one, especially in places with large Amish populations, like northern Indiana, where most churches would approve an identical Ordnung.

The Ordnung that Joni later showed Bill was only a few pages long, and it spoke in broad terms about rules of community life. But some of the most obvious and important aspects of Amish life have become so culturally entrenched that they are not even mentioned. The Ordnung said nothing about driving with horses, for example, yet, as even a casual observer can discern, horse and buggy is a defining requirement for nearly all Amish churches: Start driving a car and you are potentially excommunicated. The Ordnung also said nothing about sermons being spoken in Pennsylvania German.

The language barrier was another aspect of Amish that Bill knew nothing about. When Bill asked Joni how he would be received in the Gladwin Amish church if he were to attend a service, Joni said, "They'd welcome you, but you wouldn't understand anything because we preach in German."

Bill recalls the moment of learning about German language sermons as a big letdown. "I just accepted it," Bill says. "I thought, okay, well, this life is good for you, but it won't work for me, and God, you will have to open up something else for us." Bill prayed. He said, "God, you are leading me here and showing me there are Christians that believe the same way I do. Please open the door and show me something that will work for us."

Thinking back to those first encounters with the Amish, Tricia recalls Bill coming back to the cottage with lumber and talking about an Amish guy he'd met. "I'd think, Whatever. These Amish people, aren't they cute. That was just a different world and a different life, and I didn't want to go talk to that man, and I didn't think they'd want to talk to me," she says.

Even when she eventually went with Bill and met Joni and had good chats with his wife, Barbara, Tricia still didn't consider the Amish life as one that lay ahead for her family. "I just thought, These are the people we are getting our lumber from," she says. And even when Bill came home with the statement of faith and said, "This is what we believe. Why can't we join a church like this?" the couple just thought, Well, you can't become Amish, and they left it at that.

Eventually Tricia had what would turn out to be a fateful encounter. She was chatting with a woman who was working at the nursery at a home-school gathering near Detroit, and in making conversation, Tricia told her about the Amish work crew that was building their home in the Thumb. The woman said, "You ought to meet my friend. Her family is becoming Amish."

The woman gave Tricia the couple's name and phone number, and she shared it with Bill. "He was terrified about calling because he was worried it could be life-changing. He was afraid of what it could mean for us," Tricia says. Torn between doubt and curiosity, Bill didn't call right away. But eventually he mustered the courage, and the families met. "They had like five or six kids, and we had them all over for dessert," Tricia says. Bill and the husband hit it off immediately, and Tricia and the wife did okay too. "We didn't have a really warm relationship, but she gave me some patterns for head coverings," Tricia says. The family was moving to an Amish community in Manton, a small farming town about three hours north of Detroit.

The couple shared a piece of information that immediately caught Bill and Tricia's attention: The Manton church offered service in English every other week. Bill thought, well, maybe that would be enough.

"That is when we first said it out loud," Tricia says. "We said to them, 'We thought you couldn't become Amish.' And they said, 'Oh, yes you can.'"

Bill and Tricia couldn't have foreseen it at the time, but the language barrier they were concerned about at the very start was a hurdle they could never quite overcome, and later, fifteen years into the Amish life, struggles with the language forced the Mosers to make one of the most difficult decisions of their lives.

The Barn-Raising

For Bill, a big day in the Amish journey came when Joni invited him to a barn-raising at his sawmill. Bill felt Joni's invitation showed that he respected Bill. "I thought at the time that it was quite a privilege, quite unusual to be invited," Bill says. "It showed me that he was taking me seriously."

The barn-raising happened on a weekday, which is common within Amish communities. "Everybody is expected to drop what they are doing and come help. They call them work bees or frolics or barn-raisings," Bill says. The entire community understands the need to show up and help, and is very supportive. Later, when the Mosers had become Amish and had a bustling business making wood shipping pallets for a large Amish pallet distributor, if Bill had a midweek work bee to attend, he'd just call the distributor and tell him there would be no pallets that day and the distributor would just say no problem, understood.

For Joni's barn-raising, the whole Moser family stayed at the family cottage and then drove over to the sawmill in Gladwin first thing in the morning. Bill was excited and a little nervous. "It was one of those things where you go and everybody stares at you wondering who you are, like what are you doing here?" Bill says. After all, they were the only people not dressed in the traditional style of the Amish. But at the same time, everybody was friendly and welcoming. Bill guesses there were at least sixty men, with women and children added to that—maybe 150 people, maybe more. Both as a builder and as somebody contemplating this lifestyle, Bill was hyper-aware of the scene: the tasks, the teams, the assignments, the materials, the tools. He drank it all in.

Joni had the project extremely well planned. He had the materials prepared and laid out. He had a job foreman to run the day's work. Bill doubts the foreman was paid. Nobody else was. Joni's church is Old Order Amish, and thereby required the use of hand tools—crank drills, hammers—for the most part, but they did allow a radial arm saw powered by a gasoline engine. "And there was somebody running that the whole day," Bill says.

One construction technique that the crew used caught Bill's attention. The barn was mortise and tenon, meaning the beams fit together with a tongue and a slot, but instead of using giant, solid beams and carving the tongue and slot out of the beams, they assembled beams by laminating three 2-by-8's together. Some of the laminated beams would have the middle board protrude to be a tongue, and some of the beams would have the middle board short to create the slot. "I thought, that's a modern play on timber framing, but since then I've seen that technique on older barns in Wisconsin and Michigan," Bill says.

The men were assigned into work groups, and Joni invited Bill to work with Joni's father and his father-in-law in the barn basement constructing horse stalls. "That was perfect for me," Bill says. "I had met them before, and they were friendly, and I wasn't 30 feet up in the air. I know my limitations, and I didn't feel the need to prove myself." The men worked with hand tools, and for Bill that meant mostly a hammer, pounding big nails into oak beams. Oak is an extremely hard wood, and nailing into it takes strength and technique. Not easy. "I bent a lot of nails pounding into those rock-hard oak boards," Bill says. He remembers being so impressed with the physicality of Joni's father-in-law, who pounded nails side by side with men twenty years younger and did not flag. "Really, he was stronger than I was," Bill says.

The one downside of being in the barn's lower level is Bill did not have a good view of what was going on all over the job site, which keenly interested him. But for the most vividly dramatic moments of the construction—the raising of the barn's main structural frame—everybody was called to help, and Bill remembers the excitement and drama of that stage. The frames are built lying on the ground. Amish barns tend to have peak roofs, not gambrel, so picture something that looks like what a child might draw for a house—an outline of walls and a peak roof—all made of heavy wood beams. There were four such frames, identical, more than two-stories high at the peaks, and they needed to be stood up and then supported with horizontal beams that connected them to one another.

The foreman called all the men to help. "They pushed and pulled, there were straps and poles. It was kind of dangerous, because if one of those things went, somebody could have been crushed," Bill says. But for Bill and Tricia, it was enthralling to feel the excitement of seeing the barn come together in a day with the help of an entire community focused on the project. Adding to the romance of the day, the weather was perfect. The sun shone. It was not too hot. It was not too cold.

For Bill and Tricia, one of the most memorable portions of the day arrived when everybody stopped for a hearty lunch. "Lunch was a very big deal," Bill says.

In Tricia's view, the meal equaled the scale of an Amish wedding meal. "It was all china, glass bowls, glassware and silverware, all hand-washed," she says. "It was just lovely."

The people ate in the house, in shifts, and somebody was formally calling people by turns into the house. The men sat at long tables loaded with chicken and ham, potatoes and more. They passed platters from one to the next all around. Women and girls hovered around the table, constantly ready with more food when a platter emptied. One thing that struck Bill was, despite the magnitude of the project at hand, despite the prodigious amount of work left to complete, the lunch was not rushed.

People were relaxed, in the moment, took the time to enjoy each other's company and the food being served. Bill remembers that at every plate there was a candy bar—he learned later the practice is a tradition. "It seems like a small thing, but it felt like a special thank you," he says. The lunch lasted an hour and a half, maybe even two hours, and then the men ambled back to the project and the women cleaned up lunch. Tricia has a vivid memory from the meal's end: Joni's mother-in-law carefully packed all the china into five-gallon buckets, put lids on them, set the buckets in a children's wagon and hauled them home.

The event offered a dramatic and vivid contrast to the world of construction that Bill had worked in. Men working together. Women working together. Children running around. He concedes it was a volunteer effort and community-based, as opposed to commercial, but still, he was inspired by the spirit of the people, their community cohesion, their enjoyment of one another, and their unified effort. "You can imagine that if it was my desire to be in an environment like that ... well, I was mesmerized," Bill says. "That this actually exists, not just in Little House on the Prairie books—it was such a living representation of what the Bible talks about, what a church group should be."

The Mosers stayed late, not wanting to let the event go, breathing in every last essence of that Amish esprit de corps before it evaporated. "The last thing I remember is a group of men working on the barn doors. Some people were leaving, but this group was determined to get the doors on the barn door before they left," Bill says.

And then an unexpected end to the day. The Mosers' Suburban wouldn't start. "I remember a man made a joke, 'Did your horse balk?' he said," Tricia recalls.

The bishop of Joni's Old Order Amish church walked up to Bill—Amish bishops do not dress differently than other members of the church, so he would have been attired like any other Amish man there. "He said, 'Mind if I take a look?'" Bill recalls. And the gentleman popped open the hood, fiddled with the distributor cap a bit and got the Suburban running. Bill and Tricia were grateful, naturally, but also bemused and puzzled. How does an Amish man know about the electrical system of a Chevy Suburban?

Later on, after the Mosers had made the transition to the Amish faith, the family participated in many work bees and also received help when they needed it—when building their home, when building their pallet shop—but no work bee ever rivaled the spirit and magnitude and thrill of raising Joni's barn.

The Mosers learned that a key aspect of Amish and Mennonite life is that their lifestyle and work are incorporated into their faith. "They don't want to compartmentalize their lives," Bill says. "They want their lives to be whole. We can worship while we work, and that gives a different mindset."

A Chat with
Joni Mast

On a misty day in May, I drive to Gladwin, Michigan, to meet Joni Mast. The morning is warm and humid, and dark gray clouds are troweled across the sky like wet cement, but spring life is bursting forth. New leaves, bright and electric green fleck the trees. Hay fields spread in radiant green rectangles, interspersed with fallow fields. The first sign I see of an Amish community is a young man driving a team of two stout work horses hauling a wagon of scrap wood, outer bark slabs created when a log is squared in the mill. I suspect the wood is from Joni's sawmill and headed to a woodstove. The young man pushes the horses quickly along busy highway M-18. The horses still have their thick winter fur, a shaggy golden brown mixed with a tawny white, high-stepping, fetlocks flickering in the wind and trot. The scene feels a little chaotic, a little on the edge. The young man flicking the reins, looking back repeatedly to check traffic, the wagon bouncing along, wood jostling in the back. Two pickups ease up behind his twelve-m.p.h. rig, impatient to pass, but unable to do so on the busy highway. When the horse driver reaches a driveway, he suddenly turns sharply right into a farmstead. He slows, the tension in the scene defuses. The pickup drivers hit the accelerators and roar away down the road.

Soon I see the sawmill Joni started, stacks of logs, the little office where Bill and Joni first met, the barn Bill helped build. But Joni has since given day-to-day management of the sawmill to his nineteen-year-old son and now lives and farms a mile or so away.

I pull into the drive at the farmstead of Joni and Barbara Mast. The farm is meticulous. A large white house, and nearby, a long red barn, a warren of small outbuildings, a half-empty corn crib, the ears, visible through the slats, desiccated and dull. The dirt drive arcs a path among the buildings, creating a feel like an alley among farm buildings. I see three chickens shuttling through thick grass in the ditch along the road. From somewhere, a rooster crows.

Joni steps out from a shed, which he later tells me is the machine shop, and onto the landing. He's a step higher than I am, so I'm looking up at him.

He wears a classic Amish woven, brimmed hat with a thin fabric band, a mid-tone blue shirt, denim trousers, black suspenders, a denim vest. He wipes his hands with an auburn colored handkerchief and apologizes for the grease on his hands as we shake. The diffuse light of the day bounces up into his face, and his blue-gray eyes take on a liquid radiance, set as they are against the brim of his hat, and behind him, the black opening of the door.

We walk to the house and sit at the long kitchen table. The kitchen itself is immaculate and spare. With no artificial light, the space is lit only by the soft gray sunlight able to make it through the thick clouds and into the kitchen windows. Joni's wife, Barbara, joins us, sitting at the far end of the table, and three young daughters hover nearby. Joni is friendly and thoughtful and chooses his words.

"I never gave it a thought that Bill would be interested in the Amish life," Joni says, when thinking back to those early conversations. "He came with quite a list of lumber because he wanted to build that house down by Port Huron, and he asked me for a price and I figured it up."

Even when the two men started having conversations about religion, Joni didn't pay it much mind. "You see, there are a lot of people who ask those questions, like Bill did, and you try to answer them, and you don't see them again or they kind of fade away, so that's why it didn't seem to be important," Joni says. But after a few conversations that seemed to go deeper than typical curiosity-seeking, Joni began to realize Bill was dissatisfied with where he was spiritually and was looking to do something different with his faith.

Joni concedes that he had concerns for the Mosers. "It's kind of a hard way to go," he says. "You are bucking … well, downstream is easy, and that's kind of how we like to do as people, but especially with a family, that makes it more difficult." But Joni was impressed that the Mosers were taking their journey slowly, cautiously. He had seen others over the years who decided quickly to cross over into the Amish life, and it generally had not gone well. He recalled another family who had become Amish about the time Bill and Tricia were considering the change. The family decided quickly, joined a community but didn't stay long enough to become a part of it, left, joined another community, and then another and moved on. "Then they kind of drifted out," Joni says.

For Joni, there was a certain satisfaction in seeing that Bill and Tricia admired his faith and life so much that they would consider adopting the lifestyle. "Jesus said we should be the light of the world, and it was satisfying that people from the outside could see there was something here more than just a culture or a lifestyle." But Joni cautioned the Mosers, too, about the challenges ahead.

Nonresistance, for example. "Amish don't take up arms, and I remember having some concerns about that, wanting to make sure Bill knew where we stood on that," Joni says.

He especially wanted them to be clear and honest with themselves about their motivations. Of human nature, he says, "There's a rebellion in us … we don't like people telling us what to do, to get right down to it," Joni says. "We don't want to go away from the church we have just because we don't want them telling us what to do."

Reflecting on the
Amish Church
Service

The first Amish church service that the Moser family attended was in Manton, Michigan. Their friends the Kuhns, who had recently crossed over to Amish from general society, had moved to Manton, and so the Mosers had a connection there. At this point, Bill and Tricia were in their late thirties and had five children, the youngest, Matthew, a baby, the oldest, Tristan, ten. Tricia had not yet begun wearing a head covering.

As Bill thinks back on that first service, he remembers how struck he was by the separation of the men and women in the service. "It really made a huge impression," he says. And his feelings were mixed. On the one hand, he appreciated the separation and understood its effect in dialing down the boy-girl distractions that happen in typical church services. "In that way it was kind of refreshing," he says. But on the other hand, the Mosers were very family-oriented and much enjoyed sitting together in church. The separation was an especially big change for Tricia, because, while Bill stayed with four boys, just she and Sarah were on the other side of the church. But the couple viewed these kinds of pros and cons simply as all part of the transition process.

The Manton service was held in German, and the church provided a translator for the Mosers. Bill concedes he was in a state of checking things out, excited by the newness of things, and the German was intriguing. "And actually it still does intrigue me, the fact that the Amish could retain that language for the many years they have. We struggled with it over time, but I do understand the effectiveness in preserving faith and family and community when surrounded by a separate, complex culture."

But as much as Bill and Tricia were there to survey the all of it, the most important element they were looking for was a community of faith, and as Bill sat watching the men and women file in, the men in their black pants, white shirts and vests, the women in their dark green prairie style dresses and white caps, and take their seats together on the long benches, the thought was blossoming in his mind: This is possible. "That was the overwhelming feeling," he says. "This is possible."

As strange and as different as the service was, "when it came to community of faith, what we were seeking was right there in front of us," Bill says. "And the people were so friendly to us." The Amish do not actively recruit members, so the sense of welcome and kindness the church members expressed did not spring from a desire to close the deal on a new member, but was simply an expression of who these people were in their hearts. Bill's reaction, his thought of "This is possible," was based in good part on the support he suddenly understood would be present if the Amish community welcomed his family into its embrace.

A gentleman named Earl Chupp was Bill's translator during that first Manton meeting, and he has stayed a friend of the Mosers all these years. Regarding the service being in German, Bill remembers thinking that, as long as there would be a translator, he would be okay—he could deal with the German.

"I wanted it to work," Bill says. "And I had that feeling that the support network would be there. It was exciting, but not in a giddy way. I was still trying to maintain my head, look at the ups and downs of it." For her part, Tricia was still more cautious, but the couple was open to one another about their feelings. They knew the different ways they approach things would naturally affect how they proceeded down this path.

The sense of true possibility was exciting for Bill, but he had made a commitment to himself and to Tricia that he would keep an analytical mindset and not jump into anything. Supporting that view were the leaders of the Manton community, most notably Alfred Gingerich, who advised caution. "He was not saying, 'come away from the world and join us,'" Bill says. Alfred is careful not to overly influence seekers in trying to convince them to join the Amish. "His reasoning is he does not want to get in God's way," Bill says. "It's a big change for a family, and he sees what's at stake." Alfred's advice to the Mosers was simple: Count the cost of the change. He said this repeatedly.

Later on, after they had become Amish—first in Ovid and then in

Marion—the Mosers found special richness in the days of Amish communion. For the Amish, the communion ritual is not a standard part of Sunday service, but rather a twice-a-year event that is imbued with great devotion and is especially regarded as the time and place where community of faith is expressed and reinforced. For the Mosers, who were so propelled in their spiritual quest by a desire to find a community of faith, the days of communion were rich spiritual affirmation of the choices they'd made to enter the Amish faith and culture.

A thing to know about Amish communion is the day of communion involves long hours of devotion. In both the Ovid and Marion churches, the service would begin about 8:30 a.m. with extensive readings from the Bible, starting at the beginning and progressing chronologically with readings of long passages. Bill appreciated that the ministers would choose passages that built context and perspective when juxtaposed with one another, like prophecies from the Old Testament that were then reinforced by events that came later. "The Old Testament is full of old prophecies, pre-revelations of Christ, and our churches would have focused more on that," Bill says. "For example, in Isaiah 53, written a thousand years before Christ, there's a description of Christ's death on the cross. Our church would have focused on those types of things." The readings would proceed until about noon, when people would break briefly—a half-hour at most—for lunch.

Typically the lunch food would be kept simple. "There would be a table in the back of the church room, and it would have maybe noodles and "church peanut butter" sandwiches (peanut butter mixed with marshmallow cream, sweet pickles, pickled beets, and bread), or carry-in lunches that each family would bring, simple things, very light," Bill says. "For us, that was a very precious time spent as a family, we really enjoyed that," Bill says, thinking back on when his children were small, to a scene when maybe one child would have been on his lap; Tricia would have been holding another one, the other children would have been clustered close. And equally important, they would have been surrounded by people who shared their ideals of faith.

After lunch, the reading would resume and continue until about 3 o'clock in the afternoon. Amish ministers plan that by 3 o'clock, they are reading about the death of Jesus, and they target that time for those passages because it is thought to be the time of day when Jesus died on the cross.

Next, the congregation would break bread. "We'd read scripture about breaking bread, and we'd stand, and a bishop would go along and hand each person a piece of bread," Bill says. The bishop would also hand each person a cup of wine, refilled as needed by a deacon. The bread-breaking portion of the service would last maybe 45 minutes. The feet-washing portion of communion would happen next.

The ministers would first read scripture about feet washing, recalling Jesus's clear directive to do so: "If I then, your Lord and Teacher, have washed your feet, you also ought to wash one another's feet. For I have given you an example, that you should do as I have done to you." For the Amish, who adhere to a plain interpretation of the Bible, this statement could not be more clear, and they tend to look at Christian denominations that have abandoned this practice as examples of people explaining away Jesus's clear message and following their own path instead.

In the Mosers' church, the deacon would set up tubs of water, two for the men and, in a separate room, two for the women. The people would then pair up, a man with another man, a woman with another woman, and when their turn arrived, they would go where the wash basins were set. Each person would wash one person's feet, and as each man and woman took turns washing another's feet, the congregation would sing hymns. When a pair finishes the feet washing, they stand and greet each other with a holy kiss. "It's a beautiful service," Bill says.

Why does it work? How does such a simple and low act transform into a high point of faith and community? "You are going up with somebody you know fairly well, somebody in your community. You take your socks off. He takes his socks off. And you literally wash each other's feet, and then dry them. It's not splashing a little water on, it's washing their feet. You touch his feet with your hand. And he touches yours." The process is humbling, and making it more so, in many Amish churches, including the Mosers' Marion church, members had to bend at the waist to do the washing, which was intended to make the act even more humbling, the physical act of bowing to a community member.

"I will never forget the first time we practiced that," Bill says. "It was very powerful. It brings us together in a way that reinforces the whole community aspect, the whole 'church as community' idea, makes the community more intimate, more personal, more real."

In the weeks leading up to communion, the community works to resolve outstanding issues, the idea being that it would be hypocritical to share communion if there was strife or conflict among members. People who are known to have sinned would be expected to admit their sin and ask for forgiveness. People who have disagreements with each other would be expected to talk things through in the presence of other members and have the conflict resolved. Ministers would interview each family to make sure issues are resolved or that unresolved issues are brought up. "If we are not united, how can we have communion?" Bill says. When issues involve primarily women, ministers' wives would generally help intervene.

If conflicts cannot be resolved, the communion is not held, and if three communions in a row are not held, bishops from the broader fellowship might be brought in to assist in bringing about church harmony. But of course, the Amish are a people like any other, and none of this is perfect. In large, well-established church communities like those in Pennsylvania and Ohio, communion is nearly always held without fail. "There the concern would be the districts are just sweeping problems under the rug," Bill says. But if the pendulum swings too far the other way—withholding communion service until every single differing view is reconciled to the point of unanimous agreement—then the community cohesion can be damaged. But taken in total, communion serves its mission, in Bill's view, providing a means of restoring relationships and faith and keeping the congregation together.

Evolution to Amish

Bill and Tricia do not remember one particular conversation, one particular moment, when they decided to live the Amish life. The decision evolved as they checked out a couple of different communities looking for the right fit and the right sense of welcome. The couple knew they couldn't make the change to be Amish until they found a community to be Amish in.

The first community they investigated was in Manton, Michigan, the tiny northern Michigan burg where the Kuhn family had moved when they crossed over from general society into Amish. The Mosers would visit the Kuhns and sometimes spend the night. "We would park the van and live as they lived," Bill says. "We'd use their horses, be like them." Sometimes Bill would visit alone or with his three oldest boys. By that time, the Mosers and the Kuhns were friends, and their boys had also become friends, so sometimes they'd just visit not so much for research, but just "for the sake of friendship," Bill says.

But the Manton church itself was undergoing some struggles. The church had originally been formed as a plain, horse-and-buggy church not affiliated with the Amish—there are many versions of horse-and-buggy communities across North America. Early on, "Some of the members in Manton were, for lack of a better word, anti-Amish, people who wanted to live a plain lifestyle but were opposed to certain Amish ways," Bill says. Over time, some members wanted to join with Michigan Amish churches, and other members wanted to go in a different direction. Eventually some people left, and the people who stayed in Manton chose to join the Michigan Amish fellowship. This kind of upheaval and drama would be a big deal for any church, but in tiny churches made up of thirty families or fewer, the situation is very up close and tense for all members. After only a year, the Kuhn family left the Manton church, but not only because of the upheaval. A main reason was they could not overcome the barrier of the German language.

Despite seeing the Kuhns leave Manton, the Mosers remain indebted to them in their journey. "I can't stress enough how their example helped pave the way for us," Bill says. "We could look at them and see how they were accepted and say, yes, this could be done. Without that, I don't know that we would have had the courage to do that on our own."

The arc of the Manton church—as it moved from horse-and-buggy non-Amish to horse-and-buggy Amish, as it decided where it would fit on the scale of liberal to conservative Amish communities, as it ministered to people who were deciding whether they agreed or disagreed with the direction, as some people left, as others stayed but changed—revealed an element of fluidity and instability within Anabaptist communities that would come to play an unexpected and challenging role in the Mosers' lives.

The idea of disruption seems at odds with a people who outwardly appear so firmly fixed into a clearly defined set of beliefs and practices, a people with institutionalized resistance to even small changes in lifestyle. And certainly there are large and stable communities of Amish and other Anabaptist people. But there is a principle of Amish faith that in some ways can naturally lead to disruption. The Amish churches that the Mosers were a part of prefer no more than thirty families in a church. When a church exceeds that number, the members decide who will leave to start a new church. In theory, the new church would operate nearly identically to the church it springs from, but human nature being what it is, a new church can also be an opportunity to take a slightly different path. Also, with the notion of new churches being a baked-in part of the Amish experience, it's easy for church members who are unhappy with a community to view starting a new church as a ready and viable option to reach for when they disagree with their church leaders' decisions.

Bill and Tricia were aware of Manton's state of transition, but the couple still felt a strong need to make community a central part of their faith and decided they could endure a certain amount of turmoil in pursuit of the greater goal. Bill wrote Alfred Gingerich, the leader of the Manton church, and explained that he and his family would like to join.

In his letter, Bill explained that living in Manton is what he and Tricia desired, that they wanted to belong to a church that shares faith and community. "What would you think of us coming there?" Bill wrote. To his surprise, Alfred wrote back that he did not think the church at that time was strong enough to support the Moser family in their transition. He offered the names of two other communities, in Marion and Evart, Michigan, saying they would have better resources. "But he also said that if we still wanted to come, they wouldn't say no, is how he put it," Bill says.

Early on, Bill had made a commitment to himself and Tricia that they would join a community only if the community truly wanted them to come. "And the response from Alfred was not the resounding endorsement I wanted," Bill says. It was a little perplexing to Bill at the time, but looking back on it, he understands that Alfred had encountered a number of seekers over the years and had a better grasp of what the Moser family's needs would be than Bill did at the time, and of course Alfred better understood what his own church was going through and what it needed to weather the internal changes. Bill concedes it was something of a letdown.

Bill phoned the bishop in Evart, a man name Omer. Bill knew Omer, appreciated him as an individual and as a man of faith. "But in that conversation nothing clicked," Bill felt. Meanwhile, Tricia was pregnant with their sixth child, Jacob, and getting far along—not the best time to launch a major change of life based on an uncertain welcome. The Mosers decided not to visit Evart. "I just couldn't get up for it. We put it on the shelf again, and we continued to live our lives in the Thumb," Bill says.

Along the way, their friend Tom Kuhn suggested they contact a church in Ovid, but Bill held off because he'd heard that the Ovid church was more on the fringe of Amish practice, but six months went by and he says, "I felt I just had to do something." For all that time he had carried a name and phone number in his wallet, for a minister in Ovid named Roy Yoder. Bill called him. "He was immediately very comforting, very engaging, very dynamic," Bill says. But even Roy Yoder was not especially encouraging to the seeker Mosers. He suggested that Bill and Tricia check out a church he knew about in Flint, much closer to the Moser home. The women in the church wore head coverings, and the church doctrine was more closely aligned with the Mosers' beliefs than was the church they were attending in the Thumb. By then, though, Bill and Tricia had spent time in Manton, had seen what it meant to live fully immersed in a community of faith, and they knew that's what was right for their family. They could not back off that vision.

Roy and Bill picked an October Sunday when the Mosers would visit the Ovid church. Bill's only encounter with the Ovid congregation until the visit had been the phone conversations with Roy, a man Bill describes as "almost cosmopolitan" in his extroverted nature and welcoming of outsiders, so Bill expected a similar warmth from the people in the Ovid congregation. The Mosers and their five children headed over in the van on the appointed Sunday morning. The church meeting was at a farm that had a half-circle drive that wrapped around the barn and house and back to the road. Bill pulled in, drove around the circle and parked at the front corner of the barn. The moment is tattooed into Bill's memory because the scene was far from the gracious community embrace he'd envisioned.

About thirty or forty men and boys—from children to fifty-year-olds—all dressed in plain attire, the men in longish hair and long beards, stood in a big clump right near where Bill parked the van. In the moment after Bill turned off the engine, Bill and Tricia paused and looked out the van windows to survey the scene. Tricia said, "Bill, they're all staring at us … and they are not smiling." In a traditional Old Order Amish church, the men and boys stand in an orderly circle and greet one another prior to church service. But Ovid was, in the realm of Amish churches, a little more free form, and this pre-church gathering was just kind of a milling around, a shapeless bunch. To Bill, the group of men and their staring, unsmiling faces translated more as a mob, not an angry mob, but, say, a skeptical mob, and certainly not a warm and welcoming mob.

Among the Amish, "there's always curiosity about who will crawl out of a van," Bill says. But perhaps because he was self-conscious, or perhaps because many men in the group did not know the Mosers were coming, "seeing those people was totally the opposite of the feelings I had talking with Roy." And even as Bill worked his way through the group shaking hands, the vibe he felt was more like, What are you doing here? "I just had this sinking feeling of, oh no, what are we getting ourselves into?" he says. Luckily for Bill and his family, though, the group warmed to them, and as the day evolved, those chill feelings thawed. "And of course Roy was there," Bill says. "And he was welcoming."

Looking back on that day, Bill says some of the skepticism he felt from the group of men likely grew from the particular orientation of this Amish church. Oddly enough, the Ovid Amish church had as a central tenet the mission to do faith outreach to other Amish people. "Sadly there are Amish people who are immoral, who have a life in which they are in bondage to alcohol, sexual immorality. They are Amish because it is what they grew up with, it is all they know, and they have some vague belief in the back of their minds that it will help them get into heaven," Bill says. Bill learned that the Ovid Amish hoped to help wayward Amish see what Christ had done for them and reconnect them to a true Christian life. In essence they were missionaries, but instead of reaching out to, say, homeless people in New York City, they were reaching out to people the Ovid congregation viewed as apostate Amish.

The Ovid people told Bill and Tricia that if they were looking to live the Amish lifestyle more in a cultural sense than in a faith sense, then the Ovid church was not for them. "They said if you can help us in our mission and are looking to grow spiritually, we would welcome you."

Despite Bill's urge to quickly join a plain, faith-based community, the Mosers visited Ovid for a year and a half before they decided to move there, in part because the community seemed to still be finding its own way, defining what it would allow and not allow in practice and worship. Some members of Ovid were practicing things that in a spiritual sense wouldn't have lined up with an Anabaptist view of Christianity, and Bill and Tricia wanted to see how the issues would all shake out. "Those were red flags to us," Bill says. "But each time one of those things arose, it was eventually resolved, and it seemed the door opened again."

For example, one minister accepted elements of Pentecostal religion, which involves speaking in tongues. "For Pentecostal people, much of their spiritual experience is based on emotions, and they believe that speaking in tongues is evidence of the spirit living in you. I think that whole emotionalism could open you up to spiritual darkness," Bill says. Eventually the minister who accepted the practice was "silenced," that is, not allowed to speak as a minister. For the Mosers, that meant issue resolved.

Another issue for Bill and Tricia was that some families were fans of Christian rock, and the Mosers wondered if it would make its way deeper into the community. "I don't want any part of that," Bill says. "If other Christians want to use that kind of music, they are free to do that, but I'm free to not be a part of it." Eventually the families who enjoyed Christian rock music left the church.

What's more, Tricia is more cautious by nature than Bill, and she needed more proof that the direction they were heading was the right one. "We did a lot of talking at night about processing this change," Bill says. "She knew we had to make a change, but I remember conversations when I'd tell her, I don't see any other options than something like Amish. And I remember her saying, 'There must be other options besides doing something as dramatic as joining an Amish church.'"

When Bill thinks back on this time, searching so hard to find a faith community in which to make a home for his family, he says, "I just felt like it was dragging on and on. I felt like this should be easy to do, just do it. But it didn't feel that way at all. It felt like some force was working against it, like I was literally pulling on a physical force. I just remember thinking over and over again, Why is this so hard?" But in some ways, he concedes, the answer might be obvious, simple: it's difficult to move from one culture to another, and when you add in the Christianity aspect, the spectrum of individual interpretations of the Bible, the change becomes that much more difficult.

It didn't help that some close friends of the Mosers were doctrinally opposed to Anabaptist teachings, saying that it constitutes spiritual bondage, that the community controls you. "We of course saw it as a scriptural commandment that we submit to one another, open ourselves to advice from other Christians that we live close to," Bill says.

When the Mosers finally moved to Ovid, many of the community of faith benefits they'd so longed for and the lifestyle changes they'd envisioned were realized, but the challenges of their journey did not necessarily lessen, as they faced upheaval in their own small church.

The First Days of
Amish Life

T he Mosers finally decided the time had come to make the move that they'd thought about, anguished over and talked about for years. But how would they sell the unfinished house? By now it had electricity, but otherwise virtually all the interior finish work, including the kitchen and plumbing, remained undone. Bill called the real estate agent who had managed the land contract transaction when they purchased, and explained they wanted to sell. To Bill's amazement, the man said he had been showing a couple around the area just a week or two prior. They had driven down the Mosers' road, stopped and looked around. The client had pointed to the Moser home and said, "I would like something just like that." The agent called the couple back, explained the house was for sale, explained it was half-done, and asked if they'd like a walk-through.

The shoppers came and looked at the house. "We had a woodstove, an old one that was Fisher brand, and their last name was Fisher, and that was a huge thing for her especially—it really convinced her that this was the house for them," Tricia says. "They were just in love with the house from the beginning." They made an offer, and Bill and Tricia accepted. The couple appreciated the look of the home so much that they talked with Bill about his vision for completing it. They took notes.

A few years later, the Mosers stopped by unannounced because they were in the area. The man happened to be home sick with shingles, and the house had that unkempt look of somebody home sick, but nonetheless, he was willing to let the Mosers walk through. Gratifying for Bill and Tricia, he had truly carried out Bill's design.

Looking back on the transition—the nearly miraculous and instant finding of a buyer of a half-built house on a back road in Michigan's Thumb, the coincidence of the Fisher name, the carrying out of the design vision—Bill and Tricia see evidence of the hand of God ushering them down their chosen path.

They closed on the sale, rented a U-Haul, packed the van and drove one-hundred miles west to the tiny farm community of Ovid, about a half hour north of the state capital, Lansing. And despite the thousands of hours of prayer, thought and discussion Bill and Tricia had had alone and together, Bill couldn't completely stifle his fears as he drove the loaded U-Haul down the freeway. "I remember thinking, This is it. We're finally doing it. But also thinking, What am I doing? This is totally insane."

It didn't help that the Kuhns—the friends who had crossed from general society to Amish previously—had given up on Manton by then and had moved to a Mennonite community.

Renting the big truck and loading the van enabled the Mosers to move in one trip, which Bill saw as important to helping the family transition. "We wanted it to be definite. We are here," he says. When they pulled up to the house they were renting, a group of people were there to help them unload.

The relocation was definite, but the transition to the Amish life of horses and buggies and no electricity was more gradual. For one, the house they rented was just a normal house, a three-bedroom ranch along a state highway, with electricity and everything. "We were free to use the electricity, which is common in Amish communities if you are renting, though using the lights is discouraged," he says.

Bill even continued to drive a pickup truck for a while. He was finishing up construction jobs for a contractor near Detroit, and he asked church leaders if he could continue to drive to the job sites. They approved; it was an important concession because it gave the Mosers financial stability. Bill was at the time slightly amused at how community members also enjoyed that the Mosers had a pickup truck, asking him to move things, convey materials and people. "I remember one night after a church service, it was late, and a bishop's brother, who was in a wheelchair, needed a way home, so they just wheeled him into the back of the pickup, and a couple of his nephews sat back there with him, and I drove them home," Bill says.

Bill kept the truck about six months, but the family began going to church by horse and buggy after about a month, after Bill got comfortable enough with controlling a horse to feel safe hauling his family around that way. The community also made other concessions to make the Mosers' transition easier. Most important, they approved Tricia home-schooling the children—a practice she'd come to cherish because it brought her so close to her children. Amish communities generally don't allow home-schooling because they view school as an extension of the church, and they believe so strongly in community and feel that childhood bonds forged at school are an important part of community strength later in life. (Eventually all of the children except Timothy did attend Amish school.)

As for the change in clothing style: "Not a big deal," Bill says. "We just got our clothes." Women gave Tricia dresses. Joni's wife gave Sarah—four years old at the time—a dress her daughter had worn. Another woman made Sarah three new dresses: one for everyday use and two for church. Along the way to Amish assimilation, Bill recalls some awkward moments. For example, within some Amish communities—including Ovid—women are not allowed to part their hair. "That was a no-no," Bill says. Tricia didn't know about that particular nuance, and Minister Roy had to tell her. "It was hard for him because he personally didn't really care about it, but he knew it was an Amish thing."

As general guidance, Minister Roy just advised the Mosers to watch the other church members and "do things the way they do." Overall, the Ovid community was more relaxed than many Old Order Amish communities when it came to conformity. By contrast, nearby Manton "is very strong on everybody conforming, looking like each other," Bill says. The men's hats, for example, are all identical, purchased from the same source. "For some Amish, that is a very big thing, that people could look at you and know what fellowship you came from." In Ovid, people had more flexibility, not only in hat choice, but in things like shirt fabric, collar style, and other areas of dress.

If anything, what with living in a normal house and still having the pickup truck, Bill was struck by how the lifestyle change wasn't all that big. "I actually remember being a little disappointed in that," he says. But he appreciated, for Tricia's sake, especially, that the transition was gradual and that the community never exerted great pressure to conform immediately.

In the Amish commitment to be separate from general culture, conformity in appearance is a powerful element in the equation. Amish attire, like any uniform, immediately conveys two essential messages. One, "We are together." Two, "You are not part of us." And the attire alone establishes a kind of perpetual barrier between the wearer and people of general society. But like any human endeavor or Biblical interpretation, the notion of conformity in attire can be looked at from a couple of perspectives, Bill says. "From my own personal observation the desire to conform can be both spiritually and non-spiritually motivated," Bill says. From a spiritual standpoint, conformity suppresses the desire for individualism and reinforces the idea that you are giving yourself to a group of people, in this case a group of Christians, and you blend into that group. Strict rules for uniform dress also prevent fixating on such worldly issues as style changes. (Although Bill concedes, "there are fashion trends among the Amish, believe it or not.")

On the other hand, there can also be pride in the notion of conformity itself, pride in how perfectly one can adhere to the standard, and pride is a feeling that Amish admonish their members to avoid. So, pride in perfecting the Amish look can be analogous, say, to how a proud military officer might obsess about the shine of his buttons, the perfect placement of his medals, the crisp crease in his pant leg. "It's a constant point of tension in plain churches," Bill says. People must be aware of their motivations. "Do we feel good because we obey the rules or do we believe in the heart and obey in service to God?"

Shortly after the Mosers moved to Ovid, the congregation decided that the church had grown large enough to split into two churches, what they called a north and a south district. The Mosers decided they wanted to be in Roy's district, so they chose the south. But in the background, additional pressures were at work within the church, fractures formed over leadership and lifestyle restrictions. Differences arose between the leadership and the Michigan Amish Fellowship. The fractures widened over time and eventually the disagreements led to the church disbanding five years after the Mosers joined. They remained Amish, but moved to a community in Marion, Michigan, a couple hours north.

"It was tumultuous, but I can say there was never a point where we were in despair or really discouraged. Our faith is in God, and man will disappoint us. In large part we took things in stride and put trust in God. Let him open doors, close doors. That is how we operated to keep our courage up," Bill says. And despite the ups and downs the Moser family endured while living in their first Amish community of faith, the experience only solidified the Mosers' resolve to live in that type of setting. "I see it as a scriptural command that I cannot live apart from that, no matter how bad it gets, I have to be part of a community; living in a community is living out being part of Christ's body, his church."

Bill and a Horse
Named Rex

Bill grew up in a suburban Detroit neighborhood. He and his three brothers had mini-bikes when they were young, motorcycles when they were older, snowmobiles all the time and, like every other youth around Detroit, cars the moment they turned sixteen. Tricia never had mini-bikes, motorcycles or snowmobiles, but she did get a car. The point is, neither Bill nor Tricia was ever known to get around by horse, and they knew nothing about horses when they made the transition to the Amish life.

Maybe at some level traveling by horse and buggy might appear to be safer and simpler. After all, you are only going about ten miles an hour and there's no engine or electronics to worry about. But horses, of course, are living, sentient beings with minds of their own. They can be stubborn, they can be unruly, and, most dangerously, they can spook and bolt. When your young family is bouncing along the side of a highway in a buggy, hitched in a most literal way to a horse, there's an element of uncertainty that can play on the mind. For Bill, even after fifteen years, handling horses never felt entirely natural, and by then he'd had good reason for his qualms.

Bill admits that he was a little naive about the full implications of what going to a horse-and-buggy lifestyle would mean from a horse management perspective. "I really didn't worry too much about it," he says. "I figured we'd deal with it when we got there."

The Mosers' first horse, which they bought from friends in the Thumb, was of the Haflinger breed. The breed is smallish, more like a big pony, and the horses are known as good-tempered, hard workers. The Mosers arranged to buy a young horse at first, but the family, coming from a more complete understanding of horses, offered a better plan. "They offered us their mare, the mother of their herd," Bill says. She was about twelve years old and was very calm and easy to manage. The horse's name was Sugar, and she was the horse that the family's children drove to school. It says a lot about the Amish family's sense of giving and concern for the Mosers that they would give up such a cherished horse.

But an Amish family needs more than one horse, and soon the Mosers picked up a second horse from a family that was leaving the Manton Amish church. The Mosers traded an old fifteen-passenger van "that had a lot of miles and some issues" and a thirteen-year-old original Macintosh computer for a horse named Rex that had once been a racetrack trotter. The swap presented an odd juxtaposition that stayed in Bill's mind, one family joining the Amish life, another family leaving the Amish life.

To help get Bill started driving his horses, one of the younger men from the Ovid Amish community came over and showed him how to hook the smaller horse to the family's large double-seat buggy, and they took it out on the road. The Mosers had moved into a rental on a pretty busy highway, M-21—the family's dog was hit and killed by a car the first day they moved in—and that road is where Bill's first horse-driving lesson took place. "We just drove down the shoulder and I even made a U-turn," Bill says. "I remember thinking, This is kind of an easy deal."

Regarding that first lesson, just taking the horse out on the highway, Bill says, "I didn't know enough to be afraid." But he later heard people chastising the young man who took Bill out on the highway about how unsafe that idea was for a total novice. Shortly after, another man came over and gave Bill a more thorough lesson. They hooked up the bigger horse and traveled quiet dirt roads. "He showed me how taut to keep the reins and other things, and he was a little more nervous with me driving. You can imagine, these guys who have handled horses their whole lives suddenly in a buggy being driven by some yahoo."

Bill never fell in love with horses. He liked the idea of having them as part of his life, but more from a function standpoint, working with them, driving with them, farming with them. "I was reading Small Farm Journal, and it was pumping me with dreams of making a living with a horse," Bill says. One horse trait in particular formed a barrier to ever fully embracing them, being entirely comfortable with horses: they can shy at things, and you never know when they will do it or what will cause it. The trigger could be, say, a dog running from a yard, but it could also be something as benign and everyday and stationary as a garbage can sitting along the road. A horse can suddenly veer into the ditch, or worse, out into traffic. "I had a few accidents and that tends to kind of … it made me a little nervous," Bill says.

Bill's first accident happened not long after he started driving a horse and buggy. He was going down a big hill and looked down to notice a nut had come off a U-bolt that connects the shafts to the front axle of the buggy. He figured if he could keep just the right tension between the horse and the buggy, the bolt would not fall out until he hit the flat at the bottom of the hill. But somehow the horse was picking up on the fact that something was wrong, and he was getting nervous, wanting to run away from the problem, whatever it was. When they reached the bottom of the hill, Rex did what Bill had feared he'd do: he tried to speed up. Bill pulled back on the reins to hold him back, and then the U-bolt fell out, and the buggy started to fishtail wildly down the paved road, going about ten miles an hour. The ride ended when Rex headed into a ditch, with the buggy fishtailing along behind. The buggy flipped onto its side. Luckily for Bill, Rex stopped the moment the buggy tipped over. Bill remained in the buggy, with the battery for the road lights on top of him, and ended up with some bruises, but the accident broke two wheels on the buggy and tore the canopy. Naturally Bill thought the obvious thought: it's a good thing the family wasn't with me.

Not too long afterward, though, the family was on a horse cart when things went wrong. Bill, Sarah and the three oldest boys drove to a neighbor's to buy hay for the horses. They chose to use Sugar that day. She had been pregnant when they bought her, and her foal was a few months old now. Mares don't like to be away from their young foals, but if the absence is brief, as the hay-fetching trip would be, things usually go okay.

"Everything was going fine," Bill says. "Then when we were about an eighth of a mile from home, Sugar heard her foal in the pasture and she just bolts, goes into a full gallop." For a bit, even that was okay, because the hay cart was riding well, just going fast. Bill figured they could ride it out until she reached her foal. But as she turned into the driveway, a corner of the flatbed hit a tree. The horse had so much momentum the impact tore the entire bed off the wagon and Bill, the children and the hay all went flying. "I ended up landing partially on Sarah, but luckily she wasn't hurt and nobody else was either," Bill says.

Tricia didn't see the accident, but knew something was wrong when she saw, out the kitchen window, Sugar racing by with the wagon in tow, bouncing way too fast and nobody on it. "I about had a heart attack," she says. And she ran out the front of the house to see everybody sprawled out on the ground.

"There was that very scary moment there, wondering if anybody had been hurt," Bill says. The thing is, Sugar was the very, very safe horse that the previous owners had allowed their children to drive to school. Timothy, who would have been about ten at the time, "had some choice words for me," Bill recalls. The family had been living Amish for only about nine months at the time, and Bill and Tricia recall it as one of those moments when they thought, What have we done?

The most dramatic horse accident happened with Aaron, who was about fifteen at the time. He was farming, driving four workhorses pulling a disc harrow—called a "disc" in daily speech—through a field. When driving a disc you either stand or sit on a seat mounted above the disc. Aaron was sitting, and as he was driving, the horses suddenly broke into a gallop through the field, and in trying to slow them, pulling hard on the reins, bracing against the seat, the seat snapped off the disc. Aaron was suddenly bouncing dangerously along in the field with four giant galloping workhorses in front of him and the blades of the disc behind him, with no seat to balance against. The horses headed to a swamp at the edge of the field, and just as they reached it, Aaron slipped to the mucky ground. The horses stopped in the mud, but the disc still came forward over Aaron. But luckily the ground was soft enough that he sunk into it, and the disc stopped before running completely over him. Miraculously, he escaped unharmed.

But of course, the accidents were the exception not the rule. The Moser family figured out how to get around by horse, and luckily nobody was ever injured along the way. And to be sure, Bill did have moments when he enjoyed the horses. His favorite work with horses was raking the hay after it was cut. "There was no sound of an engine because the machine is ground-driven," Bill says. So it was just Bill and the horses and a beautiful sunny day, moving in that timeless horse pace back and forth across the field.

Bill questions whether people who do not experience horses at a young age can ever develop the sixth sense needed to become a good horseman. The chemistry is very nuanced and complicated, he says. "A horse responds to firmness, but a calm firmness. They hate pain and do not respond well to harshness, but at the same time you have to show a sense of command, that you are the boss." Bill thinks he has a hard time hitting that balance point. He's either too harsh or too lenient. "They know who a horse person is," he says. His sons, who grew up with horses, developed that sixth sense. "They are fairly skilled horsemen," Bill says.

Still, anyone working with horses can never let down their guard. Consider this horse story from *The Budget* newspaper, which posts short weekly updates from Amish, Mennonite and other Anabaptist communities around the world. This story is from Narvon, Pennsylvania, in the January 14, 2015 edition.

"A runaway horse belonging to David Mark and Rebecca King took off just as the mother had loaded the three children, ages 5 years, 3 years and 8 weeks, in the carriage. The buggy went over Rebecca's foot and she was left behind as the horse took off galloping down their long gravel drive onto Hammertown Road, down a steep hill, turning left onto Valley View Road, flipping the buggy on its side, ejecting the 5-year-old, who was picked up by a passing motorist. Help was soon there. The three children escaped serious injuries, but one has brush burns. They were soon united with their mother when someone went to get her and bring her to the scene. The horse was standing at the scene when help arrived and was not injured. The carriage was set back up and the horse and carriage driven back the two miles by a neighbor."

Tricia and the New Skill Set

A time that looms large for Tricia when she thinks back on her family's transformation to the Amish way of life is when they first stayed for a number of days in an Amish home. As planned, the visit was going to be just an overnight, a stay with a longtime Amish horse-and-buggy family that lived in Manton, a couple of hours from the Moser home in Michigan's Thumb. But when the Mosers were driving, their old Chevy Suburban broke down about halfway to Manton.

"We talked about what we should do," Tricia says. "Should we call my brother and ask him to take us home? Should we call the people in Manton to take us there?" It seemed both a practical predicament and a metaphorical moment: push forward or turn back? They called the people in Manton. The Amish family recommended a driver they knew, and he came and picked up the Mosers. Then Bill and Tricia learned their car would not be fixed for five days.

The Amish are intentionally separate from general society, and that might give the sense that they are standoffish and cold, but their culture is extraordinarily social and welcoming once you are inside it. Tricia fondly remembers that sense of gracious hospitality from her family's impromptu stay at the Amish family's house. At this point the Mosers were a mom, a dad and five young children, and the Amish family simply welcomed them without question and made them feel at home for a five-day stay.

Tricia immediately connected with the wife and felt comfortable in the home. "She is my kind of person," Tricia says. But more broadly, Tricia and Bill were captivated by how the community pitched in. The Amish people were sending over food for dinners, desserts even, just to help out because everybody in the small church community knew the Mosers were staying longer than planned, and the host family would need some assistance. For Bill and Tricia, wanting a community of people who shared their view of the Bible, people who supported each other with daily acts, this was an enchanting and vivid example of what they yearned for.

On the Sunday of the Mosers' visit, the man of the house had to figure a way to get all the Mosers to church by horse and buggy. And he did so happily, sourcing an extra buggy and horses. "He put the women in one buggy and the men in another buggy," Tricia recalls. It was late November, and "his wife was so worried about how warm I would be. She wrapped a scarf around my chin and we had big, warm buggy blankets."

The visit also left a big impression on Tricia because it was the first time she had an up-close look at the new skill set she'd have to develop, the new systems she'd have to consider, to master, if she were to actually take the step of becoming an Amish mother.

The family they stayed with lived in a new home. It was well built, clean, neat and designed for an Amish lifestyle. That meant it had things like a giant pantry, propane lights, a sink near the back door so people could wash up from farm work as they entered the house. Tricia inspected the wringer washer. She studied the pantry. "Her canning room was so impressive. It was spotless. And it was just loaded with food," Tricia says. Jar after jar of pizza sauce, tomato juice, meatballs, raspberry pie filling … the inventory went on and on. Tricia had not grown up with a family that canned food. "I don't even think I'd made bread yet," she says. Tricia also noticed that the woman was sewing underwear for her daughter, modest underwear that, in Tricia's view, fit with scriptural principles of modest dress.

And there was the garden. At this point, Tricia and Bill had had only one big vegetable garden ever and were still unsure of their ability to produce food on that scale. On a visit earlier that fall, the woman whose home the Mosers were now staying in had toured Tricia through her beautiful and bountiful garden, which was the source for her well-stocked pantry. "I asked her how she knew what to do each day in the garden," Tricia says.

The woman said, "I just go to the garden and look, and if the pickles are ready, that's what we are doing that day—pickles."

The moments, examples, comments were small, simple, everyday kinds of things, but they opened Tricia's eyes. The woman's examples showed Tricia that she needed to learn a new skill set, a daunting thing, yes, but the visit also introduced her to the possibilities of what she and Bill could achieve as a couple and as a family.

Later, after the Mosers had made the transformation to Amish, after they'd sold their house in Memphis, Michigan, and moved to Ovid, the lessons for Tricia continued, and the sense of community proved itself real. "The women were so welcoming to me in Ovid," she says. One woman who was about seven years younger than Tricia and had "bundles and bundles of energy," visited often and became a mentor. "She was a lifelong Amish woman, so even though she was younger, maybe early thirties, she had done these things her whole life," Tricia says. And since the woman's children were old enough to pitch in, she would just bring them along, and the two families would work and play together.

She taught Tricia big, important garden things, like how to maintain the fertility of the garden despite growing crops in it year after year. She taught Tricia little nuanced garden things, like how to easily achieve better spacing of carrots.

"Carrot seeds are very tiny, and they stick to your hand when it gets sweaty, and it's just difficult to get them spaced right. So she'd put a small amount of carrot seeds in a bowl and then mix them with a handful of sandy dirt and then sprinkle the mix into the row."

The woman showed Tricia how to quickly snap green beans. How long to cook them for canning. The woman told Tricia which pressure cooker to buy. She made Tricia's first true Amish dress, instructing her along the way. She taught Tricia how to sew men's pants. "We made all the boys' pants together," Tricia says.

Even though Tricia had sewn for years, she had a hard time remembering how to make men's pants, forgetting certain steps after her mentor friend had left. "There are no instructions written for making Amish clothes," Tricia says. "You just ask somebody to show you or you go ask your mom."

Tricia's friend moved so fast and used so many little shortcuts that, when she left, Tricia says, "I couldn't remember anything." So finally Tricia told her friend she had to slow it down, and Tricia would write down every single little step. "Like the pocket on men's pants is a little funny, the way you fold it a certain way, things like that," Tricia says. Years later, when Tricia would run into the woman, she'd ask Tricia if she still used the written instructions.

Making dozens of jars of applesauce was one of the first big canning projects Tricia recalls. "I had maybe four bushels of apples," Tricia says. She set a day aside. "Just setting up for it is kind of a big thing," Tricia says. You get a big bin and fill it with wash water. You get different sized pots for the various stages. And then there were unexpected little points of peer pressure about applesauce. "In Ovid, everybody said applesauce had to be white, but I don't mind the brown. Who cares what it looks like? People are so funny," Tricia says. When multiple families get together to can as a group and there are even more apples, like eight or ten bushels, there is a separate work bee the day prior called a snitzing party. The women call in the youth and they quarter and core all the apples in preparation for the canning.

The hardest skill, and one that Tricia decided she wasn't going to try to master, was butchering. "I'm not a meat person. I know I need meat for protein, but I don't really like it that much anyway," she says. So, her interest wasn't there to begin with. But with a husband and six children, raising meat was a given. The Mosers raised cows and pigs and chickens. Like canning, butchering would also often take place as a group activity. "Somebody else would be in charge and my family would be there pitching in," Tricia says. Like a barn-raising, like canning, work bees for butchering became another rich example of the community gathering to serve one another and to practice their faith in that way.

For her part, Tricia concedes that the only part about butchering she was okay with was wrapping the meat. But she didn't escape all of what she considers the gross parts. "Chickens are the worst," she says. "It's just a disgusting thing to butcher a chicken." The day would involve the men outside killing the chickens and plucking them. Then the men would bring the birds into the butchering area for the women to process. "They're just slippery and slimy, and you have to cut them a very certain way, and it's really easy to accidentally cut into the stomach, and then you have this huge nasty smell. I just can't handle it," she says. These days Tricia prefers to go to the store and buy her chickens.

"If you do butchering together it can be a lot of fun," Tricia says. "But it is a lot of work, and it is usually more than one day because after the butchering you keep on processing and putting up a lot of stuff in cans." Tricia doesn't have a problem with the killing of animals because she sees the purpose in it. That perhaps helps her be okay with some of the other visceral parts of butchering. She recalls one of her first butchering experiences, in which three or four families gathered to butcher some pigs. "They laid cardboard on the floor and taped it down, because you have blood and guts all over the place," Tricia says. She was surprised to see the extent of the meat canning. "And they really used all the parts of the animal. It was really impressive," she says. They canned meatballs, fully cooked. They canned meat patties, partially cooked. They canned raw meat—that takes an hour and a half in the pressure cooker.

At another gathering to butcher a pig, Tricia watched as a younger couple, both people skilled in butchering, took apart the animal and again used every part. "The woman took the intestine, turned it inside out and washed it. Then she stuffed it for sausage," Tricia says. The Mosers never took their butchering that far. "We just buy our sausage casings," she says. And still, when she eats sausage, Tricia peels off the casing and sets it aside.

Tricia long ago left behind her feelings of "how am I ever going to keep up with these women!" Now things like canning and making bread and sewing Amish pants and dresses are all second nature. Equally important, maybe more important, is the sense of community and faith that is interwoven with work in an Amish community, the feeling of togetherness and sisterhood that rises when women gather in a common project.

Doing Business the Amish Way

One fact the Amish community enjoys sharing is that 95 percent of new Amish businesses are still operating after five years, whereas only 50 percent of typical American businesses make it five years. The statistic is based on research by Amish anthropologists Donald Kraybill and Steven Nolt, published in their book *Amish Enterprise*. Having lived in the Amish community for fifteen years—five years in Ovid and then ten years in Marion—and having bought, sold and started a number of businesses in that time, the Mosers have seen up close the ways of the community that enable businesses and families to succeed.

The core reasons get back to the idea that the Amish are not guided by political ideology, and so the success formula involves both conservative business values and communal care values, a deep ethic of self-sufficiency and even entrepreneurialism (although Bill says the Amish would not use that word and might even reject that idea as prideful or individualistic) and a near socialistic cultural ethic to help other Amish families achieve a healthy standard of living. So, America's right wing would cheer the Amish for encouraging their children to start businesses and thereby take charge of their financial future and independence. But that same group would be repelled by an ethic, a way, they'd label as anti-American and socialistic: "It's a goal of the communities that we've been in that nobody is super rich and nobody is really poor. There is some measure of equality. Nobody is really hurting and nobody else is raking in piles," Bill says.

What's most curious and even perhaps amusing about the tremendous disparity between the Amish business success rate and that of general society, is the group completely fixated on financial success—American entrepreneurs—is failing at such a higher rate than the group who views financial success as simply a way to fund their truly important work, which is celebrating the word of Jesus and sharing that mission with the people in their community.

The Mosers' first glimpse of Amish business ways came when the family made its original transition to the faith, moving to the community of Ovid. Bill was wrapping up work on a final construction project near Detroit and looking ahead to how he would make a living as an Amish father with a wife and six children. He had considered building pallets in a small outbuilding on his property and then learned that a man in the Ovid community had just such an operation and was hoping to sell it and move to a different community. The operation was small, simple, just what Bill had been envisioning. Bill and the seller agreed to a price for the equipment and the man did not really add anything to the selling price for the value of the business—unlike standard American business deals where the seller would calculate value for the equipment and additional value for the customer base.

But the most surprising difference happened at the meeting when Bill and the seller were finalizing the deal. The seller perceived that Bill was not entirely aware of how much money he would need at the start to purchase a stash of lumber—raw material to make the pallets. "So he said, 'You will need $10,000 to get it going, so I will just keep $10,000 in the company's bank account and you can just pay me back as you are able to,'" Bill says. "I was astonished by that. He initiated it, and there was nothing written down." If the deal had transpired according to standard American business rules, Bill is not sure the enterprise would have survived.

Over time, Bill saw that the way the pallet business transaction happened was not unusual, especially when the transaction happened among church members. "You hear a lot of that kind of testimony, and that was the teaching we had," he says. "If you have extra money, you make it available to people who need to start a business or a home."

Another key difference Bill found between the typical American way of business and the Amish way was a remarkable willingness to share business information, even among people who would be considered competitors from a general society viewpoint. So when Bill first bought the pallet business, he was able to go to other Amish people who were also building pallets and talk with them about how best to run his new business.

That knowledge not only helped him survive the early days, but also helped him see possibilities for the future, identify important equipment to acquire. "We visited two pallet shops in Ludington (about 150 miles from Ovid), and that information is just shared freely, it's just considered a social time," Bill says. The owner of one of the shops explained how a more advanced nailing machine dramatically increases production, how it can be remarkably cost-effective and was a good investment. Bill made a mental note that that machine would propel the next step of his business, and it did.

When the Mosers later moved to an Amish community in Marion, Michigan, they saw similar support from the Amish. A large pallet distributor in McBain, about ten miles north, offered to purchase all of the equipment Bill would need to start making pallets with automated nailing equipment, a forklift, and generators, and the Mosers would only have to build the pole barn and pour cement for the loading area. What's more, the pallet distributor in McBain would purchase all of the pallets the Mosers could make. After about five years, the McBain pallet distributor approached Bill again, this time offering to fund a significantly larger machine and new building. The Mosers had to secure a loan for the expansion, but the equipment had so much production prowess and was so efficient that the profits enabled him to pay off the loan very quickly. Of course there is vulnerability in having one customer, but given the Amish ties, the business relationship remained strong, and the Mosers had a thriving family business. I could imagine a traditional American businessperson reading of this type of situation and thinking, "Well, anybody could succeed if they could do business that way," and I suppose that is the point.

When deals involve buying a farm, transactions can take many shapes, Bill says. A seller might finance a portion of the farm at very low interest or even no interest and then have a balloon payment that would come later. If the seller happened to be retiring, he would likely have a desire to help somebody else get started farming and do what he could to enable that. Whether a deal involves land or business, there is a shared desire to keep the asset in the community. "If somebody has a farm and they sell it outside the community, there's a feeling that you've kind of lost that land, especially in places like Marion where there is strong competition for the farmland," Bill says.

But even in the Amish community, not everybody owns a business or a farm. Yet in the communities where the Mosers have lived there has existed an ethic of helping ensure that employees can be okay financially. The Mosers' Marion community had a successful sawmill. The business, though small by American business standards, is not structured in the common way of a single owner who hires people at, say, $10 an hour, while keeping the larger profits to himself. The principal owner pays the workers $15 an hour and adds bonuses for performance and shared ownership as well, so they can benefit from the profits. The employees can also earn ownership, that is, they do not have to put money into the deal to become part of the ownership team. Some people, Bill explains, do not want the responsibility of ownership, but with the wages higher than what's common locally and bonuses on top of that, they are able to get by in the rural Amish way.

Farming is another area where Bill has seen cooperation among people who general society would view as competitors. The local foods movement is a situation where the world has come to the Amish door. They have grown their foods with organic, sustainable practices for generations and have centuries of shared knowledge about growing produce. The enhanced interest in local foods means more Amish can make a living that way, which helps to slow a long-term trend of Amish having to leave farms because they are not able to make it work financially. Bill has seen people who are expert produce farmers offering advice to other Amish farmers. "They are essentially helping a competitor get started," Bill says. "I know spiritually how it works. If you bless somebody, you will be blessed back, somehow, some way, the good you do will return to you. But I know there must be some business principle involved there too, even outside the spiritual or community aspect. I have to believe there is a principle there that works."

Sunday Morning at the Amish Church in Marion

On a sunny but chill November morning, I drive to farmland outside Marion, Michigan, to attend church service in the Mosers' former Old Order Amish community. Like most Amish communities, the Marion congregation meets in member houses, and the house where I'm heading today is the same house where the Mosers first shared church service with their Marion neighbors a decade ago. I had arranged the visit with one of the church leaders, so the congregation was expecting me, and two translators were ready to whisper real-time translation to me throughout the three-hour service.

I turn down a dirt back-road that's washboarded and muddy from recent rain and pull up to a spacious white home with a white barn and outbuildings set close by. The buildings are well kept. The farmyard is tidy. Several black buggies and horses round out the scene.

Before Old Order Amish service, men and boys typically gather outside or in an outbuilding, like a barn, to greet one another and chat. Often they will stand in a large circle until it is time to head inside for the service. As I arrive, the men and boys have just broken from the pre-service meeting and are walking into the home. From youngest to oldest, the males all wear the classic Amish Sunday attire of black pants, white shirt, black vest; the men wear brimmed black hats. One by one, as they reach the door to enter, each removes his hat and sets it on a table that stands on the porch beside the door. Soon, a sizeable jumble of brimmed black hats is piled in the soft light of the November morning.

A minister greets me in the sunny yard and explains that one of the translators will show me my seat, but the conversation is brief because the minister has to go finish preparing for the service. He introduces me to my translator, who shakes my hand, gives a warm smile, and we walk inside. Bill tells me Amish are generally open to visitors curious about their church service, but he suggests a phone call ahead of time to arrange.

A fundamental tenet of Amish faith is to reject the notion of a large and powerful church hierarchy. There is no national or international leader who speaks for the Amish people. There is not even a national governing board. The Amish are committed to community and brotherhood, committed to one another in an intimate way. And one way this is expressed and reinforced is to meet in people's homes—modest spaces lacking distractions and thereby focusing attention on the message and the people in the room. [Some Amish congregations do meet in simple churches, but the majority retain the home church custom.] There are no soaring ceilings, no stained glass windows, no images of Jesus, no gold crosses, no crosses at all, no robes, no elevated pulpit, not even a small podium on which to put papers, because the ministers must speak without notes.

In other faiths, elaborate and beautiful architecture and iconography are celebrations of the Creator, but to the Amish, they become barriers, distractions from the focus on what matters: an intimate sharing of Jesus's message with the men, women and children in their lives. The only overtly religious thing I see in the room where the Marion congregation meets today is a sign above the family's coat rack that says, "In all things give thanks."

The term "plain" refers to people who choose to live low on the technology scale, but the term is also perfectly apt for the place of today's worship. Plain. The room is well-built, solid, tidy, warm, and large enough to hold more than a hundred people, but also the room is plain to its soul. The floor is cement. The walls and ceiling are entirely covered in 4-by-8-foot panels of OSB, also called particle board or chip board. The congregation is sitting inside what is essentially an OSB box with a cement floor. The OSB is not painted. The boards are nailed to the wall just as they came from the store, complete with the logo of the manufacturer stamped in about a 1-foot-square imprimatur in the middle of each sheet. A wood stove warms the room, and a fire extinguisher hangs nearby. A kitchen sink, dish-drying rack on the counter and set of cupboards sits in a corner. A bottle brush and a hacksaw hang on the wall above. A wringer washing machine stands nearby. The unpadded wood benches have no backs, and the congregation settles onto them for the entire three-hour service.

The men file in and take their seats on one side of the room, the left side when facing front. Young boys sit with their fathers. Teen boys and girls sit up front near the ministers, younger married men sit at the back of the room. I sit in the row second from back, and a translator sits directly behind me so he can speak quietly directly into my ear. The women then enter from a separate door, walking single file down a staircase—each one, from youngest to oldest—in long dark-colored dresses—green, blue, brown or gray—and white caps.

As everybody gets settled, when there is still no leader at the front of the gathering, and not a word has been spoken, a man from a bench somewhere in the middle of the room sings—in a clear, strong tenor—an opening line to an ancient hymn. The congregation joins in song. The language of the hymn is a German dialect called High German from the 1500s, and different from the Pennsylvania German that Amish people typically speak. Bill compared the difference between High German and Pennsylvania German to the difference between Shakespearean English and today's American dialect, "or maybe even more different than that," he said. The tune is very slow, and the voices of men and women and children gently rise and fall in slow harmony. The congregants sing for a while, then the singing stops. There's silence, a brief pause, and then the tenor from somewhere in the middle of the men leads with another solo line, and the singing begins again. Slow, and chantlike, similar to Gregorian chants, but not as soaring, but also not mournful. Still, the songs run in minor keys, and the sensibility is pious, sober, devout, beautiful and musical and deep, and the overall effect is a kind of musical meditative state.

The hymns come from an ancient German hymnal called *The Ausbund*, and many of the book's songs were written by fifty-three Anabaptist prisoners who were held in the castle dungeon of Passau, Germany, from 1535 to 1540, awaiting execution for their Anabaptist beliefs. The songbook handed to me for the service has English translations of the songs, but the translations are more in the vein of direct translations, not singable translations, so the songs are for the most part locked in High German.

Bill tells me later that the second song sung, called "Das Loblied," or "The Praise Song," is the second song sung in Amish services at the approximately 2,000 Amish congregations around the planet. The song's fixed role in Amish church service gives it a cultural significance in addition to its religious significance, serving to connect Amish people to one another across time and place.

I write the first verse of The Praise Song, song 131, pages 328 and 329 of my hymnal, and later see it sung on YouTube videos, copied on web pages and appearing in several books about the Amish, so important is it to the faithful:

Oh God Father we praise You
And your goodness exalt
Which You, O Lord, so graciously
Have manifested to us anew
And have brought us together Lord.
To admonish us through Your Word
Grant us grace to this.

The singing continues for a half-hour in this way. An individual will sing an opening line, and then the group joins in. But there is no discussion between songs, there is no choral director, no obvious leadership. The song stops. There is a pause. A man sings a line and all then join.

I take it all in. The plain space, the slow, chantlike songs, the uniform dress, the sense of community so palpable in so many ways, but especially in the way things happen with only the slightest clues and no overt sense of leadership. (Bill and Tricia explain to me later that the song sequence and the leader of each song is all decided and assigned ahead of time.) The Amish have been starting their meetings like this for hundreds of years, and that feeling of something that transcends centuries is evident on this day. The gathering feels soulful and beautiful and rich and full of faith. It is counterintuitive that one of the most profound religious services I've ever witnessed is happening in an OSB box with a cement floor and not so much as a single cross visible, but such is the case.

A somber sense of order prevails, but everyday humanity is also on display in the background. A woman stands with a baby and walks up the stairs. Soon another woman with a baby does the same. In front of me, an older man appears to doze in a rocking chair, one of only a few chairs in the room. Near the window, a younger man, maybe in his early thirties, also appears to be dozing. Another man combs his hair, singing the whole time. A girl of about two, dressed in a jewel green prairie style dress and white cap, stands and wanders along the knees of women seated at the benches; nobody seems to mind. A baby cries. A little boy yawns. The boy next to him stares out the window. Another young boy rests his chin on the edge of the wringer washer and stares at me. For the most part, the younger boys don't sing. And through it all, the choral singing continues, the slow, slow songs, the slow rise, the slow fall. The song abruptly stops. Another pause. Another lone voice sings a line. The song starts once more. The sound resonates in the big OSB box, and the music works its magic, transcending time, reaching way, way back.

After a half hour of singing, six men walk down the stairs that the women entered on. The men walk to the front of the room and sit on a bench. One of the men stands to begin the sermon. He has round wire-rim glasses, a gray-white beard and hair. The translator whispers the minister's words in my ear. He speaks of helping, of bearing one another's burdens. "But don't look at this as a burden," he says. "It is part of God's plan for our well-being."

He tells the story of the foot washing at the Last Supper and that Jesus said to "do also to one another."

"I am glad we do this. It has to do with a condition of the heart, but it is an outward expression of brotherly relationships, when you are down at somebody's feet and humble yourself that way."

After a while a second minister stands and picks up the theme. He too has glasses, and his bushy hair and beard are as thick as steel wool. "This debt to one another is never fulfilled. We are always indebted to love one another," he says. Then he reminds them of the commandment. "Jesus said to love your neighbor as yourself."

And finally a third minister speaks. His beard is long and gray and reaches to mid-chest. "A man who walks in the ways of the Lord is like the wind, a quiet force," he says. And later, "We need to be a chosen people. You are a peculiar people; the world does not understand us." He shares a story of going to a child's funeral, and on the way he saw a rainbow. "Is that not a promise?" he asks. And as he does so, he starts to cry and stops to blow his nose, wipe his eyes, and gather his composure. "The fear of God is the beginning of wisdom. It is better to receive punishment when we don't deserve it than to reject punishment when we do deserve it." And toward the end of his talk he says, "It's a privilege to have this today. We are not worthy of this privilege. And we are privileged to live in a land where we can practice faith as we believe."

As the service nears its end, the third leader asks the gathered to pray on their knees. They slide off their benches and bow their heads to the seats. Many of the men wrap their arms around the tops of their heads. The prayer ends and people slide back onto the benches and the final song begins. Again the long, slow chant, but this song slightly brighter, slightly more uplifting and a strong sendoff for the congregation. By now it is noon. During the three hours, clouds have blown in, dropped snow, dropped sleet and just as quickly blown out. Now the sun shines again, and on the clothesline out the window I can see hundreds of beads of water running along the ropes, each drop glistening in the sun, an adornment at today's cathedral.

A gentleman tells me the congregation is staying for a special meeting that is for baptized members only, and that I'm being asked to leave. Understood. I file out the door with the young people, who are also not baptized—and won't be until they make the conscious choice, generally in their late teens or early twenties. I head into the November day and walk to my car.

Connectedness

One of the biggest surprises I had as I spent time talking with Bill and Tricia Moser about their Amish years is how they had become connected to what seemed like a multitude of people not only within their community, but also all across the nation. I had assumed that being Amish meant leading a simple, quiet life cocooned inside a miniscule community, and that the extent of an Amish family's social circle would naturally be limited by things like traveling by horse, scaled back use of phones, and no email. But I couldn't have been more wrong on that perception, and as the reality of the extent of their community dawned on me, it seemed like such a vivid counterpoint to the notion of connectedness in general society that we read so much about today.

Connectedness. The media presents the idea as if connecting to people is a new trend, and that the way it exists is through, say, clicking "like" on Facebook, or sending out a photo on Instagram or typing 140 letters into Twitter. Those digital means constitute connectedness at some level, but what I saw in the Mosers' lives was a connectedness that was so much more rich because it was based on conversation, handshakes, shared meals, spending nights in people's homes and inviting people into their own home on a remarkably frequent basis. By comparison, the connectedness of our digital day could be construed as the opposite of true connectedness, a superficial layer of interaction that takes the place of human interaction and leaves us more separated because people actually come to believe it is the real thing, when in fact they are just sitting alone at their computer clicking "like" and reading posts by people they might in fact have essentially no interaction with.

I first got a sense of the Amish version of connectedness when scheduling interviews with the Mosers. So often Bill would say to me things like, "I can't that day because some friends from Missouri will be staying with us for a few days." Or "I can't that day because we are going to Maine to help build a house for a family whose house burned down." Or "I can't that day because we are going to a wedding in Indiana." Or "I can't that day because the youth group is coming to our house for singing." I came to see that somehow the only people I knew who got around by horse and buggy and did not have a phone in their house were the most networked people in my world.

"It's kind of a 'one big community thing,'" Bill says, when I ask him about his family's network. Of course a foundation for strong connections grows from practices of the faith, practices that create a kind of community intimacy—the foot washing during communion, regular work bees, and even adhering to the scriptural command that men greet each other with a light kiss on the lips. But the Mosers found extensive connections far beyond the confines of their own small church community.

They discovered that Mennonites and Amish, though likely leading very different lives from the standpoints of technology use and degree of immersion in general society, still bond over a shared belief in the Anabaptist statement of faith and even shared genealogy. "Even the most liberal Mennonite and most conservative Amish probably share some ancestry, and that usually ties back to Anabaptist time or soon after that," Bill says.

The deeply relational aspect of the faith leads to more and more connections. "Visiting is the Amish form of entertainment," Bill says. For the most part, Amish and Mennonite people build their leisure time around visiting. If they take a week off of work they do not call it a vacation; they call it a trip, because it is mostly a social journey. The family might take in some sights along the way, see an attraction or some such touristy thing, but mostly what they will do is line up a series of people to visit, and they will stay at friends' homes as they travel. For the most part an Amish family would avoid hotels and at some level, a friend who is being visited would be slightly offended if the visitor chose to stay in a hotel instead of the home. "You'd stay in a child's bedroom or a guest room, or, a lot of people we know have small guest apartments," Bill says.

To help me understand, Bill tells of a man he has met maybe three times. Bill doesn't know him well, but in those few meetings the two men really hit it off, had rich conversations. I asked Bill if he and his family were to visit that man's town, would Bill know the man well enough to stay at his house? "Oh, definitely. It would be very comfortable. And we'd invite them into our house, too," Bill says.

If Amish people are traveling through an area where they don't know anybody, they can turn to a copy of Mennonite Your Way, a nationwide directory of families that rent rooms or guest houses to travelers. You just phone the family and arrange your nights as if booking a hotel room. The suggested rate is $10 per night for adults and $2 per night for children. If you take breakfast, the suggested offering is $2 per meal.

Obviously, people in general society travel the country visiting friends too, but what's different is the extent of such visiting in the Amish world and the clear expectation that travelers would stay in a friend's house. Bill estimates that his family would stay fourteen to twenty days a year in others' homes, and people would stay in their home a similar number of days. So roughly one day in ten, for the Moser family at any rate, involves some kind of sleepover with a friend.

Bill and Tricia also came to see that the Amish and Mennonites are endlessly curious about people who join their lifestyle from the outside. Bill and Tricia's journey into the faith has led people to seek them out, invite them to share their story, and that has fostered even more connections. To illustrate, Bill shared a recent sequence of events.

The Moser family drove from their new home in Missouri to a youth meeting in Arkansas. There they met a young man, also from Missouri, who was soon marrying. They struck up a casual friendship. Bill shared his story with the young man, his journey from general society to Amish. The young man then invited Bill to speak at his wedding, which, typical of Amish/Mennonite weddings, had about 400 people. While there, Bill and Tricia met dozens of people. Later, a gentleman learned by word of mouth that Bill told a powerful story of transformation and contacted him to speak at his church, where Bill then made dozens more connections. More speaking invitations then followed.

Curiously, though, there are elements of Amish connectedness that are not entirely unlike Facebook, missives comprised of bare snippets of news and nearly anonymous conversation. The most popular such form happens in a weekly newspaper called *The Budget*. Based in Amish Country, in Sugarcreek, Ohio, The Budget carries typical local Sugarcreek, Ohio, news, but also prints brief posts, updates, from dozens of Amish, Mennonite and other plain communities around the nation and around the planet, and a very high percentage of plain families subscribe. The weekly community news items tend to be a mix of diary and neighborly news. A woman might write of the week's rain and how it is delaying harvest, then mention that she baked a pie and then ask people to pray for a community member who had a heart bypass and wrap up with a story about a church district member who had a runaway horse and another who had visitors. The entry could be from a church district in Sugarcreek, Ohio, or the plains of Manitoba or Belize or Africa. The Moser family, with their habit of traveling and visiting, have been mentioned in The Budget community news items a number of times.

Less universal, but still popular is a communal phone network in which callers phone in to group chats that run 24 hours a day, 6.5 days a week. Called The Amish Mennonite Conference Line, the system allows people to call in and share news with anybody who is on the line at the time, which could number in the dozens or even hundreds. Users need a PIN (assigned by the administrator) to access the network. According to Global Anabaptist Mennonite Encyclopedia Online, "In November 2010 there were an average of 6,000 calls per day to the Amish Mennonite Conference Line." Use peaked the day of the Nickel Mines Amish school shooting tragedy, when 1,037 callers were on the network at one time, according to the website. The chat line offers multiple conversations to join, segmented loosely by topic, like news or farming, but also just chatting. Bill says youth, too, are drawn to the group chat line as well and "it can become a time waster." Conversation happens in both Pennsylvania German and English.

Martyrs Mirror

T he Bible, and especially the New Testament is, of course, the foundation and the beating heart of the Amish, Mennonite and similar faiths, but in nearly every Anabaptist home another book also stands on the shelf. The book is titled *Martyrs Mirror* and carries the subtitle, "The story of seventeen centuries of Christian martyrdom, from the time of Christ to A.D. 1660." Though the Amish are committed to nonviolence, this cherished book is a long, graphic and deeply disturbing account of violence, chronicling as it does the killing of more than 4,000 Christians. A Dutch Mennonite, Thieleman J. van Braght, wrote the book, which was released in 1660, expanding a martyrs chronicle that had been written a thousand years prior, in 597 A.D. The second English translation was produced in 1886 and was in its 32nd printing in 2012.

Running nearly 1,300 pages and weighing in at six pounds, the book delivers a few core messages. First, it reminds Anabaptists of the sacrifices their predecessors made in devotion to their faith, in devotion to the simple and straightforward way in which they interpret Jesus's teachings. The clear implication is that today's Anabaptists must be prepared to endure hardship and persecution themselves. A second purpose is to reinforce the rejection of infant baptism and the commitment to adult baptism—a foundational tenet of Anabaptist faith. And a third core purpose is to remind Anabaptists that their predecessors, in the face of pending execution, held fast to nonviolent resistance. The victims courageously and peacefully accepted their fates and "returned good for evil" as they were tied to stakes, and flames rose around them, or as they were stuffed into sacks and thrown into rivers, or as they were shoved upside down into wine barrels filled with water somewhere in a dark, stone dungeon, or as they were simply strangled by an executioner's bare hands.

Because van Braght's history of martyrs begins in the first century after Christ's birth, many of the victims could not be considered Mennonite or Amish, because those faiths did not come into existence until the 1500s and 1600s respectively (the Amish did not form until 1693, thirty-three years after *Martyrs Mirror* was first published). Many of the book's recountings in the first century are tied to the Bible: the beheading of apostle Paul in Rome in 69 A.D.; Thomas, tortured by the natives in Calamina, 70 A.D. As the centuries play out through the book, many accounts have a short descriptive heading like this: "Arnold, a teacher of the gospel and the Christian faith, martyred in a forest near Paris, A.D. 5.11," followed by a one-paragraph description.

As the 1100s dawn, van Braght introduces a group called the Waldensians and tells many of their persecution stories. The Waldensians share many of the Anabaptist beliefs, and van Braght and other religious scholars consider the Waldensians a precursor group to the Anabaptists. But prior to the 1500s, the historical record is understandably more scant, and detail in the accounts is often brief, so van Braght covers the first fourteen centuries A.D. by page 362. The remaining nearly 800 pages are devoted to years 1500–1660, and the stories are far more detailed because van Braght was able to draw upon more solid historical documentation, like letters from prisoners, purportedly eyewitness accounts and transcripts of court proceedings. Van Braght describes his sources as "authentic Chronicles, Memoirs and Testimonies." For example, a collection of letters from the imprisoned Hans Bret, written in 1576, runs fifteen pages. Nearly twenty-five pages are devoted to two transcribed scriptural debates between Franciscan friar Cornelis and two imprisoned Anabaptists. A brief excerpt of the debate between Friar Cornelis and Herman Vleckwijk is below, from May 10, 1569. Note the Anabaptist's unwavering commitment to a literal interpretation of the Bible.

Fr. Corn. Bah, you stupid Anabaptist, did Christ then come from heaven into Mary with flesh and blood, with skin and hair, entrails and all, as He ascended up to heaven? Bah, what do you say of this, you great, stupid, awkward ass?

Herm. I do not say this; but say that the Word came from heaven, and became flesh in Mary, as John writes in his first chapter.

Fr. Corn. And we Catholics say that the most pure blood of Mary became flesh, in spite of your miserable teeth, see.

Herm. This defiance to my teeth is a small matter; but this defiance to the holy scriptures is a great blasphemy.

Fr. Corn. Ha, you damned Anabaptist, I do not blaspheme the holy scriptures; but you revile the holy, blessed, pure virgin Mary. Bah, I am surprised that you do not say, that she conceived her son Christ of her husband Joseph, as your hedge-preachers preach in the Gruthuysbosch; it is not a fine thing?

Herm. You wrong us greatly, that you say this of us; for we believe as Matthew writes in his first chapter: Joseph took his wife, and knew her not till she had brought forth her first born son."

Fr. Corn. Ah, bah! did Joseph know her afterwards, eh?

Herm. It matters not to me whether he knew her afterwards or not.

Fr. Corn. Indeed? and do you then not believe in the perpetual virginity of the blessed virgin Mary? Let us hear now.

Herm. We find nothing said in the scriptures, concerning her perpetual virginity.

When Bill Moser was in the earliest days of learning about the Amish, he remembers when he first read that it wasn't non-Christians who killed Anabaptists, rather it was other Christian believers who hunted down the Anabaptists and put them to death. "What very much struck me is that they were persecuted by the Catholics and the emerging Protestants, and I remember wondering why other Christians would feel threatened to that degree by people who professed nonviolence, who were no physical threat." Bill felt it said something positive and strong about the Anabaptists, but he wasn't sure why he felt that way.

For the 1685 edition of *Martyrs Mirror*, Dutch illustrator and engraver Jan Luyken created 104 copper plates illustrating scenes of persecution retold in the book. The most famous print still adorns the current edition's cover and is an iconic image for Anabaptists around the world. The engraving depicts a winter scene in which a man is standing on a frozen river reaching to save another man who has fallen through the ice. The story is that the man standing on the ice is Dirk Willems, an Anabaptist who had just escaped from a castle prison by climbing down a rope made of rags, and he was fleeing over the lake. The man who has fallen through the ice and who is likely about to drown is Willems's pursuer. According to the story, Willems saw his pursuer fall through the ice and turned around to save him. When the pursuer was safe, he then recaptured Willems, who was then burned alive in 1569.

Willems's story is perhaps the most famous tale of Anabaptist persecution, but, of course, it is just one of the 4,000 tales of death reported in the book. Some of the anecdotes are reported with sketchy detail, barely a few sentences—understandable given that they might have occurred several centuries prior—but other accounts offer remarkable detail, including quotes from the victims as they stood burning at the stake. While there is no way to verify the accuracy of the anecdotal accounts, accurate historical detail was possible for van Braght to establish from the court records because many of the cases are relayed in court transcripts. The executions were not the result of spontaneous mob violence or of impromptu riot battles between one religious sect and another, rather the executions were coldly official and formal affairs, sanctioned by both religious and government leaders, because when these executions took place government and religion were joined.

With government and religion conspiring to keep power, when Anabaptists rejected the government-sanctioned religion, they were also denying allegiance to the nation—committing religious heresy and national treason at once. Given the persecution that Anabaptists suffered when church and state were one, it's easy to see why separation of church and state remains a pillar of Amish belief and culture.

The original translation of *Martyrs Mirror* from Dutch into German came as a request from German-speaking Anabaptists living in the North

American English colonies. They feared their growing numbers would incite violence against their people, and Anabaptist leaders wanted copies of *Martyrs Mirror* to share and help gird their faithful against persecution. In 1742, six ministers from Shippack, Pennsylvania, wrote to Anabaptist leaders back in Europe, "It becomes us to strengthen ourselves for such circumstances with patience and endurance, and to make every preparation for steadfast constancy in our faith." When the first translation of *Martyrs Mirror* was printed in North America it became the largest book printed to that point in the New World.

Many of the cases reported in chapters covering the 1500s and 1600s are told in two parts: an anecdotal account followed by a transcript of the victim's court document. The Dirk Willems case is presented in that manner. Both portions—the anecdotal account and the court record—of the Willems case are reprinted in full below (from the second English translation).

Anecdotal account of Dirk Willems execution:

"In the year 1569 a pious, faithful brother and follower of Jesus Christ, named Dirk Willems, was apprehended at Asperen, in Holland, and had to endure severe tyranny from the papists. But as he had founded his faith not upon the drifting sand of human commandments, but upon the firm foundation stone, Christ Jesus, he, notwithstanding all evil winds of human doctrine, and heavy showers of tyrannical and severe persecution, remained immovable and steadfast unto the end; wherefore, when the chief Shepherd shall appear in the clouds of heaven and gather together His elect from all the ends of the earth, he shall also through grace hear the words: "Well done, good and faithful servant; thou hast been faithful over a few things, I will make thee ruler over many things; enter thou into the joy of thy Lord." I Pet.5:4; Matt. 24:31; 25:23.

Concerning his apprehension, it is stated by trustworthy persons, that when he fled he was hotly pursued by a thief-catcher and as there had been some frost, said Dirk Willems ran before over the ice, getting across with considerable peril. The thief-catcher following him broke through, when Dirk Willems, perceiving that the former was in danger of his life, quickly returned and aided him in getting out, and thus saved his life. The thief-catcher wanted to let him go, but the burgomaster, very sternly called to him to consider his oath, and thus he was again seized by the thief-catcher, and, at said place, after severe imprisonment and great trials proceeding from the deceitful papists, put to death at a lingering fire by these bloodthirsty, ravening wolves, enduring it with great steadfastness, and confirming the genuine faith of the truth with his death and blood, as an instructive example to all pious Christians of this time, and to the everlasting disgrace of the tyrannous papists.

Note.—In this connection, it is related as true from the trustworthy memoirs of those who were present at the death of this pious witness of Jesus Christ, that the place where this offering occurred was without Asperen, on the side of Leerdam, and that, a strong east wind blowing that day, the kindled fire was much driven away from the upper part of his body, as he stood at the stake; in the consequence of which this good man suffered a lingering death, insomuch that in the town of Leerdam, towards which the wind was flowing, he was heard to exclaim over seventy times: "O my Lord; my God," etc, for which cause the judge or bailiff, who was present on horseback, filled with sorrow and regret at the man's sufferings, wheeled about his horse, turning his back toward the place of execution, and said to the executioner: "Dispatch the man with a quick death." But how or in what manner the executioner then dealt with this pious witness of Jesus, I have not been able to learn, except only that his life was consumed by the fire, and that he passed through the conflict with great steadfastness, having commended his soul into the hands of God.

As we have come into possession of the sentence which these rulers of darkness passed upon this friend of God, we have deemed it well, to add it here for the benefit of the readers, in order that reading the same, they may be able to perceive the truth of this matter.

Court record of Dirk Willems execution:

Whereas, Dirk Willems, born at Asperen, at present a prisoner, has, without torture and iron bonds (or otherwise) before the bailiff and us judges, confessed, that at the age of fifteen, eighteen or twenty years, he was rebaptized in Rotterdam, at the house of one Pieter Willems, and that he, further, in Asperen, at his house, at diverse hours, harbored and admitted secret conventicles and prohibited doctrines, and that he also has permitted several persons to be rebaptized in his aforesaid house; all of which is contrary to our holy Christian faith, and to the decrees of his royal majesty, and ought not to be tolerated, but severely punished, for an example to others; therefore, we the aforesaid judges, having, with mature deliberation of council, examined and considered all that was to be considered in this matter, have condemned and do condemn by these presents in the name, and in the behalf, of his royal majesty, as Count of Holland, the aforesaid Dirk Willems, prisoner, persisting obstinately in his opinion, that he shall be executed with fire, until death ensues; and declare all his property confiscated, for the benefit of his royal majesty. So done this 16th of May, in presence of the judges, Cornelis Goverts, Jan van Stege Jans, Adiraen Gerritts, Adriaen Jans, Lucas Rutgers, Jan Jans, and Jan Roefelofs, A.D., 1569.

The compelling irony of an Anabaptist man turning to save his pursuer's life and then being recaptured by the man he saved and then being killed has helped earn the Willems story its iconic status, but in reading *Martyrs Mirror*, what becomes even more powerful is the piling on of case after case where an Anabaptist man or woman was killed for his or her belief. Adding to the power of the message is the perfunctory nature in which the court sentences—death and all possessions seized by the king—were assigned and carried out, all because of a refusal to renounce an Anabaptist principle of faith. A second case is reprinted in full below.

Anecdotal account of the execution of Anneken Heyndricks, A.D. 1571:

In the year 1571, there was burnt alive, at Amsterdam in Holland, for the testimony of Jesus, a woman named Anneken Heyndricks, aged about fifty-three years. Having come from Friesland to Amsterdam, she was betrayed by her neighbor, the underbailiff, who entered her house, in order to apprehend her. She said to him with a meek spirit: "Neighbor Evert, what is your wish? If you seek me, you can easily find me; here I am at your service." This Judas the traitor said: "Surrender, in the name of the king." And he bound Anneken with a rope, and led her along with him, as Judas and the scribes had done with our predecessor, Jesus. When they had arrived on the Dam, Anneken said, that they should not hesitate to look at her, since she was neither a harlot nor a thief, but a prisoner for the name of Jesus. After arriving in the prison, she thanked and praised her Lord and Creator with a humble heart, for counting her worthy to suffer for His name's sake. And she boldly confessed her faith before Pieter the bailiff and the other lords. They greatly tormented her with Baal's priests, in order to cause her to apostatize; but through the grace of God she valiantly resisted it. This greatly astonished the bailiff, that she did not pay more regard to his spiritual lords, and he said to Anneken: "Sir Albert, our chaplain, is such a holy fellow, that he ought to be mounted in fine gold; and you will not hear him, but make sport of him; hence you must die in your sins, so far are you strayed from God."

Thus they suspended this God-fearing aged woman (who could neither read nor write) by her hands, even as Christ had been, and by severe torturing sought to extort from her the names of her fellow believers, for they thirsted for more innocent blood. But they obtained nothing from Anneken, so faithfully did God keep her lips. Hence the bailiff preferred against her the charge of being infected with heresy, having forsaken the mother, the holy church, now about six years ago and having adopted the cursed doctrine of the Mennonists, by whom she had been baptized on her faith and married a husband among them. Thereupon she was sentenced to be burnt alive. She thanked the lords, and said with humility, that if she had done amiss to any one, she asked them to forgive her. But the lords arose and made no reply. She was then tied on a ladder. Then she said to Evert the underbailiff, her neighbor: "Thou Judas, I have not deserved it, that I should be thus murdered." And she asked him not to do this any more, or God should avenge it on him. Thereupon Evert angrily said, that he would bring all those that were of her mind into the same trouble. Then the other bailiff came once more with a priest, tormenting her, and saying that if she did not renounce, she should go from this fire into the eternal. Thereupon Anneken steadfastly said: "Though I am sentenced and condemned by you, yet what you say does not come from God; for I firmly trust in God, who shall help me out of my distress, and deliver me out of all my trouble." They did not let her speak any more but filled her mouth with gunpowder, and carried her thus from the city hall to the fire into which they cast her alive. This done, the traitor Evert, the underbailiff, was seen to laugh, as though he thought he had done God an acceptable service. But the merciful God, who is the comfort of the pious, shall give this faithful witness, for this brief and temporal tribulation, an everlasting reward, when her stopped mouth shall be opened in fullness of joy, and these sad tears (for the truth's sake) shall be wiped away, and she be crowned with eternal joy with God in heaven.

Court record of the Sentence of Death of Anneken Heyndricks, Surnamed de Vlaster:

Whereas, Anna Heyndricks daughter, alias, Anna de Vlaser, formerly citizeness of this city, at present a prisoner here, unmindful of her soul's salvation, and the obedience which she owed to our mother, the holy church, and to his royal majesty, as her natural lord and prince, rejecting the ordinances of the holy church, has neither been to confession, nor to the holy, worthy sacrament, for six or seven years since [but has dared], to go into the assembly of the reprobated sect of the Mennonists, or Anabaptists, and has also held conventicles or meetings at her house; and has further, about three years ago, forsaking and renouncing the baptism received in her infancy from the holy church, been rebaptized, and then received the breaking of bread according to the manner of the Mennonist sect, and was also married to her present husband in Mennonist manner, by night, in a country house; and though she, the prisoner, has, by my lords of the court, as well as by divers ecclesiastical persons, been urged and repeatedly admonished, to leave the afore-mentioned reprobated sect, she nevertheless refuses to do it, persisting in her obstinacy and stubbornness, so that she, the prisoner, according to what has been mentioned, has committed crime against divine and human majesty, as by said sect disturbing the common peace and welfare of the land, according to the import of the decrees of his majesty, existing in regard to this; which misdemeanors, for an example unto others, ought not to go unpunished; therefore, my lord of the court, having heard the demand of my lord the bailiff, seen the confession of the prisoner, and having had regard to her obstinacy and stubbornness, have condemned her, and condemn her by these presents, to be, according to the decrees of this royal majesty, executed with fire, and declare all her property confiscated for the benefit of his majesty aforesaid. Done in court, on the 10th of November, in the year 1571, in presence of the judges, by the advice of all the burgomasters in my knowledge, as secretary, and was subscribed.

One autumn afternoon I sat down to talk with an Amish couple, Alfred and Martha Gingerich, of Manton, Michigan. Alfred is the bishop of their congregation and beyond that is widely respected among the Amish for his insight. For him, *Martyrs Mirror* performs as the book's author and translators and publishers hoped it would. "I have made the statement, 'people not interested in their past have no future.'" he told me. "As a people, as a group of people, we are very much interested in what happened to our fathers and grandfathers, and on back, how they lived their faith."

For the Gingeriches, the book is a touchstone. It erases the centuries between the Amish of today and the Anabaptists who came before. Time may have passed, but the raw human experience, the devotion to faith, the unwavering commitment to nonviolence, the love of Jesus Christ, transcends the years and feels as fresh and relevant as if it were part of today. The suffering of the people, their thoughts, their letters to their families, it all feels current and reminds Alfred and Martha, and the members of their family and the people in their church, that life is not intended to be easy, and that the way of the faithful is fraught with challenge.

Martyr's Mirror also includes instances of God punishing the perpetrators of violence against the Anabaptists. The excerpt below tells of what happened to a priest who had persecuted several members of the Anabaptist faith.

"It also came to pass that the priest of the castle, N., who had so spitefully betrayed these dear friends of God, was very sorely punished by God; for such putrefaction entered his flesh, that it fell off piecemeal, or was cut off from time to time, from his body, no physicians being able to cure the disease. Thus it happened on one occasion, a large piece, of putrid flesh having dropped, or been cut off from his body, that the same was eaten by a dog, while he beheld it with his own eyes. How he must have felt on this occasion, it is easy to imagine, especially when viewing it as the fulfillment of a curse said to have been pronounced upon him. "That he should yet with his own eyes see the dogs eat his flesh."

An 8th Grade
Education

When the Mosers decided to become Amish, they did so knowing that people of the faith stopped the formal schooling of their children at the end of 8th grade. The Amish believe that close exposure to mass American teen culture after that age seriously erodes the connection their children have to their faith and goes directly against a core principal of the faith to remain separate from general society. The right to stop a child's education at such a young age was long a point of dispute in the United States, because dating back to the early 1900s, most states required that children attend school until at least the age of sixteen.

Within both Bill's and Tricia's extended family, the issue of stopping the children's education at 8th grade was the single most contentious aspect of the family making the change to Amish. Both families are highly educated: Tricia's brother is a chief financial officer of a university, Bill's eldest brother had a career with a publisher of college textbooks, and his wife had spent her career as a Ph.D. genetics researcher at the University of Wisconsin, Madison.

Beginning in the 1920s and running until the Supreme Court decided the Amish education issue in 1972, a number of school districts attempted to enforce mandatory schooling laws on Amish parents. Some local prosecutors jailed Amish parents for refusing to send their children to public school. Other prosecutors levied fines—in some cases assessed each day a child stayed away from school—and sometimes the fines would climb to tens of thousands of dollars. In many cases Amish families would tire of the conflict, which they viewed as religious persecution, sell their farms and move to a different school district or a different state that did not enforce the requirement.

The man who led the initiative that propelled the issue to the U.S. Supreme Court was Reverend William Lindholm, a Lutheran minister who, oddly enough, lives barely two miles from where Bill Moser grew up riding mini-bikes, playing backyard baseball and listening to Detroit's soul music in a working-class Livonia, Michigan, subdivision.

I asked Rev. Lindholm, eighty-one years old at the time of the interview, to share some backstory on the case. Why, as a Lutheran, did he feel the need to defend the Amish and their early termination of formal education as a means of religious expression? Which memories still shine brightest when he thinks about the initiative he led as a thirty-something minister, who was at the time working in tiny harbor towns along northern Lake Huron?

As a minister the idea of religious freedom is understandably close to your heart, but why did you feel so strongly about it as it related to the Amish and education of children?

It goes back a long way. One thing happened when I was in high school in Ogden, Iowa, where I grew up. There was an oration competition and it was based on the constitution. To get your topic you had to pull a piece of paper out of a hat, and on the paper was written something based on the Bill of Rights. And my topic was religious freedom. So I had to write an essay and speak about religious freedom.

Well, it turned out I won the district competition, and then was invited to the state competition, and I got first place there too, in the state of Iowa. And then I was invited to read the piece on an Iowa radio station, WHO, which is a clear-channel station, so people could hear it across the nation. So here's a boy from a little farm community with 1,500 people in it winning the oration competition for the whole state and reading it on the radio for everybody to hear.

So you went to college, graduated and became a pastor.

Yes, and I graduated seminary in 1958, and I became a pastor in northern Michigan. I had two churches, one in Oscoda and one in East Tawas, on Lake Huron. About the mid-'60s, I had to build a church camp near a little town named Fairview—that sounds like an Amish or Mennonite town name, doesn't it—and one day I went up to inspect the construction site, and I saw some men behind one of the buildings, and they were dressed in black and wore big broad hats, and they were speaking a funny language. I asked them if there was a historical celebration of some kind, and they said no, they dressed that way for religious purposes. I asked the foreman about the guys, and he said they were his Amish relatives from Indiana, and they were there to help paint the building.

At this time there were news stories from Iowa—we still listened to WHO in Michigan—about Amish families being forced to send their children to public school. And the stories talked about how keeping children out of school was like abusing children and was very wrong; Iowa was just polluted with this idea. My wife and I discussed it, and I said I have to go talk with these Amish from Indiana. And I talked with them for just a short while, and I was convinced the news was wrong. What convinced me is they had the right to do what they were doing because of freedom of religion. Separation from the world is central to their religion.

How did it expand from you having this idea up in northern Michigan to you plugging into something bigger?

I called Reverend Dean Kelly, who was the director of the Office of Religious Freedom for the National Council of Churches. I said that at the annual meeting we need to have a resolution supporting the Amish, but he said that would put it off too long because not everybody agrees. Some people think parochial school is wrong and it could take months of discussion. He said to me, "Why don't you do something?" And I said, "Well, what am I going to do out here in the Huron National Forest?" And he said, "Well, think about it. You will think of something."

So what did you think of?

Well I heard of this guy at the University of Chicago who had studied the issue, and he said it had gotten way out of hand, and he was holding a conference at the university. I went there, by myself, and I announced that if anybody is interested, I am having a dinner that night and you are invited to come. I just had food brought into one of the rooms at the University of Chicago. Maybe twenty-five people came, including a U.S. senator, several Amish, an attorney, and some clergy. They said, let's form an organization, the National Committee for Amish Religious Freedom. And the people elected me chairman. One of the attorneys there was William Ball, a constitutional attorney who was working for the Catholic church.

William Ball would eventually become the attorney who argued your case in the Supreme Court.

Yes. Later that year I called him—it was on Christmas Eve—and I said, Could you help these people that are being arrested for failure to participate in public school? We called him because he seemed to be the sharpest attorney working in this area of constitutional law.

Give us some background on the strategy.

When you take a case to the Supreme Court, you can't introduce any new evidence there. So you can't pick up a case that's already been tried at a lower court because the records might be incomplete or not very persuasive, so you have to know right at the start that you are taking the case to the Supreme Court so you can build the record from scratch and know that it is good. So, for example, we couldn't use a recent case in Iowa where the Amish had built their own school, because that had already been tried in court. And there was another case in Kansas where a girl said she had satisfied the requirements through correspondence school, but our attorney said that record was not substantial enough.

And all of a sudden I get this letter from three Amish guys in Wisconsin. They said, "We need help. We have been arrested." So that seemed like it could be the one, a case we could build from scratch.

What led to their being arrested?

What happened is the gym teacher had said to their daughters that you have to wear gym shorts. The Amish families said that is not modest enough for our faith, but we will allow the girls to wear culottes [baggy shorts that look like a skirt]. But the teacher and the school district said, No, you can't do that. So the Amish bought a one-room schoolhouse that had been vacant and taught their kids in there. Well, the school superintendent had the fathers arrested. We think a main reason was the state reimbursed schools for the number of students, and the school would lose money equal to about half a teacher's salary if the kids left the district. It was in New Glarus, Wisconsin.

I've read that William Ball was somewhat controversial.

Yes, well some people felt that he was really promoting Catholic schools and took the case to help the cause of parochial schools. But he had argued before the Supreme Court before, and I knew he was very capable. And he said he would take the case for free.

The Amish don't believe in suing people or hiring lawyers, which is one reason they would generally just pay fines or go to jail. How did you get over that hurdle with these three Amish gentlemen?

I drove over to meet with them in person. It was maybe a ten-hour drive, so a pretty long drive, and I was alone and thinking about what I would say to them. When I drove up into their yard it was early in the afternoon, sunny. There were a couple of buggies in the yard and some horses tied up. And, you know, it was a very strange scene for the beginnings of a U.S. Supreme Court case that became one of the most important cases on religious freedom in history. I went into the house and sat down. It was a plain farmhouse.

It didn't have any running water or electric lights, a regular Amish house. Amish houses are fairly spacious because they take turns having church in their houses. So as I remember, it was a plain, adequate Amish farmhouse.

And I knew my biggest job was going to be not before the Supreme Court, but in convincing the Amish to let us help them. They didn't want to get involved in any legal business. And there had also been an Amish leader from Iowa, a Mr. Bontrager, who asked the Wisconsin families to not go to court because if the case went against them it would be bad for Amish people all across the nation—it would settle it that everybody would have to send their children to school to the age of sixteen. Well, eventually they listened to me and not to him.

The important thing I said to them is we are not going to be suing anybody. We will just sit there and explain why we think you are not breaking the law. We will explain why sending your children to school will hurt you and your faith, and we will just tell your story. I said we are just interested in the larger picture of religious freedom. If the government can do this to them, it can do it to other people, too.

How long did you spend talking with the Amish fathers?

I'd say it was maybe an hour. They explained what they were doing and explained that their children were not going to school. They were very forthcoming, not scared or anything like that. They just wanted to know if there was anything we could do to help them. I believe we just sat in the living room. I don't remember seeing any kids.

What about afterward, on the drive home, do you remember the kinds of things that were running through your mind?

Well, everybody said the Supreme Court would never take this case. But these people came here back in the 1700s because they were being killed in

Europe, tied in gunny sacks and thrown into rivers and burned at the stake because they didn't believe in infant baptism and wouldn't become military officers because of conscientious objection. And William Penn said to them that if you come here, I will guarantee your religious liberty. And they came to Pennsylvania. And now there are no Amish in Europe and nearly 300,000 here, which says something about our country, that we have freedoms here that you don't necessarily have anywhere else. So ... they had this school problem and the school problem came up in Wisconsin and ... boom. We went after it in a big way.

Tell us about the first trial, at the local level, what did you do to make sure you had built a case that could win a Supreme Court trial.

Well, Ball wanted to show that Amish children do just fine in life with the kind of education they receive. So he put people on the stand that could testify to that. He put the county welfare director on the stand and asked him if Amish people are on welfare, and the man said the Amish are no problem to the county government, and he'd never known an Amish person to be on welfare. And he put a sheriff on the stand, and asked if the Amish were a problem for the police. And the sheriff said no, the Amish were not a problem for the police, that they are excellent citizens. And he put John Hostetler on the stand—the world's leading scholar about the Amish at the time—and he testified that if the Amish go to school the Amish faith will be destroyed because being separate from the world is so central to their faith. And he put the one Amish father and an Amish minister on the stand and they testified what they believed and why the schooling would harm their religion. And I asked that he put one of the Amish girls on the stand, and he did, and he asked her if she preferred the Amish way. So that was it. The court case was over in one day, and the record was complete, and it was as good as Mr. Ball would have liked it to be.

But that first case went against you.

Yes, the judge said that the state was violating the Amish religion, but that the state education requirement was more important, and he fined each of the fathers $5. And when we took it to the second-highest court in Wisconsin, the judge ruled the same way. So we appealed to the state supreme court. And just before we went to the state supreme court, somebody blew up a bomb at the University of Wisconsin in Madison, and it killed a graduate student, and when Mr. Ball began his statement before the court, he walked up there and said, "I want you to know that I take this case for free because I believe in it." And he said, "I also want you to know that an Amish would never set off a bomb. They only want to be left alone."

Tell how Wisconsin's supreme court ruled.

We won that one. Six judges ruled for us and only one ruled against us. So then the Wisconsin attorney general appealed to the federal Supreme Court. The state legislature passed a resolution asking him not to appeal, but he did anyway, and the Supreme Court agreed to hear the case.

Share some impressions from your day at the United States Supreme Court.

You have to have permission to go into the courtroom, so our attorney secured seats for several Amish and me. None of the Amish who were involved in the case were there, but there were Amish from Pennsylvania.

I was in awe in several ways. I was with people who were historic people. They had come here for religious freedom, and we were going up to the Supreme Court to get religious freedom for them. And if we lost, it would be a very tragic thing. We were filled with a lot of emotion as we were walking up there. For me, I was thinking, How did I get here? I'm just this young guy [forty years old in 1972] from Iowa, and here I am walking up the steps of the Supreme Court. We weren't laughing, and we were very serious and praying that things would turn out in their favor. It's ... very potent for me to think about ... and I don't know ... the Amish were quiet. And they did not say, "What will happen if we lose?" I don't know what their thoughts were, but I'm sure they'd have been like mine were if I'd asked them. They were just quiet and there to support their brothers from Wisconsin in their religious liberty and to support me. And I was there to support Mr. Ball. And he did a very fabulous job of representing. I don't really remember anything specific that he said, but I just remember feeling like everything was going okay, and it was, because we got a unanimous decision.

How did you do all this, help coordinate this case and do your job too?

Yes, well, like I said, I had two churches and it's a lot of work having two churches. I had three services every Sunday. But, you know, I was elected to do a job, kind of pushed into it, and once I was there, I just kept going. Just like I was elected chairman of the church camp committee and I hired people to run it. I didn't get paid to do any of it—I'm clergy.

The National Committee for Amish Religious Freedom still exists to this day, why?

Yes, and I'm still the chairman. There have always been problems of one kind or another for the Amish. We were in court over the slow-moving vehicle signs. And the courts agreed that it's not that great a thing ... that studies show accidents happen whether there's a sign or not. Another had to do with photo IDs. Many Amish do not want their photo taken, but today, with fears about terrorism, you need a photo ID to travel outside the country. So today there's a woman who is from Canada, living in the United States with her husband and children, and if her mother dies in Canada, she can probably leave the country but probably won't be able to get back into the U.S. I don't get the feeling that people are passing laws to do away with the Amish, it's more about people passing laws and not thinking through the exceptions.

Do you stay in touch with the Amish?

Well, I don't really have any personal friends who are Amish. But a year ago I was asked to go to meet with an Amish committee in Michigan, and I thought it was going to be a small board meeting, like eight or ten people, but when I showed up there were eighty or ninety guys there, meeting in a machine shed—a fifteen-passenger van would pull up and a whole bunch of Amish men would get out of it. And they were from all over the United States. And they were grateful to us in their mild way. They said we'd like to hear you speak, and I told them why we had gotten involved and what we continue to do with the National Committee for Amish Religious Freedom, that we want to see they'd be able to practice their way of life, that we believe in religious freedom and we believe in it for ourselves and for anybody else. It's very unusual for them to have an outside speaker, and it was very heartwarming to see that's how they felt about us.

Do you think most Americans are in support of the Amish?

Yes, I do. The United States is the best place for religious freedoms, but things still crop up.

Grandma Moser
Weighs In

W hen attorney William Ball built his case about Amish education for the Supreme Court, he called to the stand the county welfare director to testify that he was not aware of any Amish people accepting welfare payments in the county. He called the sheriff to testify that the Amish do not cause problems for the police. He had a school official testify that the students are well behaved and successful. His point in this line of testimony was to show that while the Amish education process does not look like the standard American way of schooling, Amish people are successful nonetheless and not only by their community's standards, but also by the standards of broader society.

After the 8th grade, Amish boys find work in family businesses or in the community, and Amish girls work with the women of the community to provide food and clothing for their families. As the Amish see it, the education of their children doesn't stop, it continues toward the important goal of learning life skills and weaving faith and work and family into a more seamless life fabric.

When I spoke with Bill's mom, Joyce Moser, about Bill and Tricia's transition to Amish, she said that at the time, the idea of her grandchildren's education ending at 8th grade was her biggest concern. "I thought they had to have at least a high school education to live in our world, and I thought they were depriving them of that," she says. Looking back on it now, now that four of the six Moser children have grown to adulthood, she says, "I was ignorant about the education part."

Watching her son's children grow within the Amish community has also convinced her to be less blindly accepting of the standard American school system. Joyce worked in hospital administration for decades, and she saw many sad stories of young people play out at St. Mary's Hospital, in Livonia, Michigan. "I saw children who were in public schools committing suicide, on drugs, children who had no respect for adults or anybody else. There are so many bad influences for children, they don't know where to turn. It broke my heart seeing young people ruining their lives like that."

Joyce concedes that she "is torn." On the one hand she sees the obvious reasons why people need at least a high school education in today's world. And she has several grandchildren who have gone to college and are pursuing 21st century kinds of goals. In what's one of the most extreme counterpoints possible to the Amish life, one of her granddaughters was studying to become an astronaut. But on the other hand … "I think, well, what is it they actually learn in high school? They do learn history and math and things you really need in life, but you also learn so many things you don't need."

When she steps away from those kinds of pros and cons, though, and looks simply at who her grandchildren are, who they've become having been raised the Amish educational way, she has no doubts whatsoever. "Bill's kids read so much every day, they are constantly reading, constantly learning. When I sit at the table with them, in the evening after dinner, we sit and talk, and they share their stories and ideas, and I have learned so much from listening to them. I think, They don't have a high school education, but they are some of the smartest children I have ever met. Bill's kids have so much character, and that is so important. If you don't have character, you don't have anything. And Bill's kids have the character they need to succeed."

Amish school in many ways would not be so unlike standard American rural education in, say, the '50s. Students study English and basic math and science, though evolution would not be taught. But the Moser children did perform such classic science-class activities as looking at insects through microscopes. And, yes, softball during recess. One difference would be German instruction, but the dialect taught in the Mosers' Marion school was Old German (not Pennsylvania German, which is the daily spoken language). Old German is the language the Amish Bible is written in, and would be roughly analogous to learning Old English.

For the Amish, the idea of "education" has less to do with "schooling" and more to do with "life learning" and the skills children will need to survive in the Amish culture, Bill explains. Some of that learning happens in school. Much of it does not. He runs through a quick list of things his children learned. "Doing carpentry work, milking cows, running a dairy, building pallets, running a pallet business, building rustic furniture, running a furniture business, making maple syrup at a large enough scale to produce income for the family, caring for and working with animals, training horses, driving horses …"

Turning to Timothy for an example, Bill recalls when the family first moved to Marion, and Timothy was fifteen years old. For income, Bill took on a large carpentry project, doing all the trim in a big house being built nearby, and he needed his eldest son, Tristan, to help. But at the same time, the Mosers were also buying a business that made rustic furniture, which Bill and Tricia intended to be the family's main source of income long term. With Bill and Tristan tied up on the carpentry project, fifteen-year-old Timothy—whose education was achieved entirely through home schooling—was assigned to apprentice with the owner of the rustic furniture business, learning the business enough so that he could essentially run it and then teach the rest of the family. And that's what he did.

"So Timothy was leading it, learning from the owner, and then just two weeks after Timothy started, the guy says, 'Oh, he knows it now, I'm leaving.' And fifteen-year-old Timothy was pretty much running the shop and the business," Bill says.

Not long afterward, as the Mosers were renovating their home near Marion, Timothy designed and installed the heating system for the house, which included in-floor heat and a wood-fired outdoor boiler, and he figured out the heat to the work shop as well. He was perhaps seventeen by then.

The Boundaries
of Technology

The first time I sat down to speak with Bill and Tricia in depth about their choice to live an Amish life it was early 2009. America had just entered a troubled time. The Dow had fallen from 14,100 to 7,500, millions of people were losing their homes, debt-fueled consumerism had veered into a very mucky ditch, and some were saying Americans were taking a new look at what's really important, about our culture possibly making a long-term change to a simpler lifestyle. At the time I was working on a magazine article, figuring I'd head to Marion, Michigan, and talk to the people who had the simplest life I knew of and ask them to tell me why they rejected today's American way and crossed over to Amish. I wanted to see what I could pull from that for people like my neighbors, the families I saw at my kids' school, the people I saw walking on the sidewalks of my town or trolling the mall, and naturally, for myself and my family.

We met at the end of January, a 12-degree morning when snow covered the ground and a brilliant blue sky opened above. When I pulled up, in addition to noting the black horse buggy parked in the drive, I saw fifteen-foot-high towers of shipping pallets rising from a paved lot near a metal pole barn. I was pondering how the Mosers stacked the pallets so high without motored equipment when the garage door opened, and one of the Moser boys drove out on a forklift. I was puzzled because I'd thought they couldn't drive things like forklifts. It was my first clue that the technology tableau of the Amish was far more complex than I'd guessed.

Bill gave me a brief tour of the workshop before we headed into the house to talk. The home business that the Mosers were running at the time was building pallets, which they sold to an Amish pallet distributor in McBain, maybe ten miles away. The Amish limit their use of electricity, but not all are opposed to mechanical automation, I learned.

I watched as Aaron, eighteen, and Timothy, twenty, loaded wood into the pneumatic pallet-making machine (the air pressure powered by a diesel engine), and then one of them pushed a button. The machine engaged and bam, bam, bam, bam, out came a pallet on the other end.

Eventually each son would have to decide on a home business of his own. Bill explained that Aaron was experimenting by selling battery-operated headlamps locally and through mail order. Of course the obvious question arose in my mind: wait, I thought that Amish people don't use electricity—why the inconsistent application?

We headed into the house, an old farmhouse that the family renovated and expanded to about 3,000 square feet. Tricia had coffee ready in a stovetop percolator. The cream on the table came from the Mosers' Jersey cow. Sarah, fourteen, was home because she graduated from Amish school last year; she's sewing something for a wedding gift. The two youngest boys are in school, a short walk down the road. Sunlight washes in through a south window that faces the road, and periodically, horse-drawn carriages and sleighs drive by.

Like anyone else in America, I'm curious about the Amish and technology. I think of the forklift, a battery-powered saw Timothy used in the shop, the battery-operated headlamp business. I think of the telecommunications network—phones—that Amish use extensively to pass news. The couple learned of the 2006 Amish school shooting in Nickel Mines, Pennsylvania—in which ten students were shot, five of whom died—within minutes of it happening, far sooner than most Americans.

And there are other places where I'm surprised to find technology in the conversation. Tricia says a newspaper photographed a story at the Montana Amish school where their eldest son was teaching at the time. "You can see it on the Internet," Tricia says. The community has not officially discussed Internet use, so the Mosers use the connection at the nearest library.

I ask Bill and Tricia to clarify the technology rules, because the boundaries seem so inconsistent: you must drive a horse, but you can charge a high-tech lithium battery with a generator? You can't use a button (most Old Order Amish communities do not allow buttons, and clothing is instead fastened with hooks), but you can use a fully automated pallet maker? You milk your cow by hand and then go surf the Web?

I'm curious not just because I want to know how things are decided for the Amish, but also because I suspect that within the Amish decision tree for technology there is likely to be guidance for everyday Americans who are contemplating how to manage technology in their own homes. From what I could tell, my friends from general society and my wife and I are all inconsistent too. (That's where "because I said so," comes in, right?) A phone for a ten-year-old but not a nine-year-old? A larger TV for the parents' bedroom, but not for the kids? An arbitrary limit on the minutes of video games a day? Why no screens on the weekend? No texting during dinner—does it really matter?

A key thing to know, Bill explained, is that every Amish congregation establishes its own technology rules, and among the 2,000-plus Amish congregations in North America there is a dizzying array of what's allowed and what's forbidden. Phones: some communities might have one or two phones for all to share, mounted in phone booths; others allow phones in workshops, but not in homes; some, but very few, allow phones in homes. Many allow cell phones—but turned off in the house. Lighting: some communities allow only kerosene lights; others also allow propane lights; others also allow bright, battery-powered lamps. Other examples: the lowest technology communities don't even allow gravel on their roads and don't allow members to mow their grass. The highest technology "horse and buggy" communities allow diesel tractors and then drive those tractors to church, pulling their families in wagons and leaving the horses and buggies at home. "Those communities are called tractor-driving New Order Amish," Bill explained. There's also the Beachy Amish (named after Bishop Moses Beachy), who allow members to drive cars. Some academics who study Amish culture do not include the Beachy Amish in their research.

In general there is limited interaction between groups who operate at different technology levels. I was surprised to learn that if somebody from a lower-technology horse-and-buggy community in Gladwin, Michigan, (where Bill and Tricia were first introduced to the Amish) were contemplating marrying somebody from the Mosers' somewhat higher technology horse-and-buggy church, the Gladwin church would discourage that union.

I ask Bill about the principles that guide the decisions. One gets back to a central tenet of Amish faith, adhering to what Anabaptists believe is Jesus's dictate that Christians live separate from general society. "In the world but not of the world," Bill says, repeating the Bible passage that Amish so often quote. "We do not want general culture to get a grip on us, and technology is a pretty gripping thing." I can't help but think of the human pose that seems to be at the periphery of my vision wherever I am in general society today: a person with head tilted down, staring at a phone in hand. I might think that, as we all stare at our phones, we too are in the world but not of the world. If we were to make a black silhouette cutout to represent the human experience of our era, that pose could be a contender. I too am guilty.

"So how much do we accept what is out there and how much does technology entangle us into a world system and society and culture that may not be our understanding of what Jesus wants for us?" Bill says.

Bill and Tricia were attracted to the idea that people could exist in a subculture that was so purposeful about how it approached technology, actually go against the flow of technology and make clear, thoughtful, committed choices about what they think is valuable. "The Amish didn't accept it as a given that the latest technology is something we need to function. They question, how will these affect a person, or how will it affect a family, or how will it affect the church," Bill says.

Despite differing technology standards among communities, a defining goal the many churches share is keeping out technology that weakens the family or the community, Bill said. Cars, for example. The decision to not own automobiles is largely a result of a desire to keep men working at home or as close to home as possible. But the Amish can hire people to drive them places.

Bill conceded that he hires drivers often to take him to Marion or Cadillac. "I'm at the upper end of the use scale," he said. He should be riding his bike—the nearest town, Marion, is just six miles away. But he shrugs it off—he is, after all, a son of the Motor City.

I asked Bill to talk through a technology decision his community had made. He chooses the issue of how propane should be supplied in a home. The community was deciding between the standard general society way (a large central tank outdoors with pipe leading indoors) or small tanks, like what you'd see attached to a home barbeque, connected to individual appliances, like a stove or a propane-fueled refrigerator, or an individual lamp. Picture it: a floor lamp, tall and spindly, connected at the base to a 5-gallon canister of propane.

Some congregation members felt if propane were piped throughout the home, it would be too easy to have a light in every room, so family members would be more likely to read in their own bedrooms and spend less time together in the evening gathered around a light in the living room. I was reminded of a mainstream woman I once knew who traced the breakup of her family to when her husband brought home a television for each kid's bedroom. I recalled another family I knew in which a son spent so much time burrowed away in his bedroom with his computer that his dad, in the heat of an argument with the boy, grabbed a screwdriver and removed the bedroom door.

The Mosers' community ultimately allowed piping of propane because of fire concerns related to small propane tanks in the home. "In a fire, each one of those tanks becomes a bomb in your house," Bill said. Helping sway the decision was a case not long prior to the church's discussion when, in another community, a young Amish mother and her baby were killed in a house fire in which a small propane tank exploded.

Many of the technology decisions that Amish wrestle with have to do with farming, Bill explained. In the Mosers' community, a member wanted to purchase a round baler for hay, which enables a farmer to harvest hay solo. But some in the community felt that the team approach to hay is an essential part of neighborliness and keeping community bonds strong. Eventually they allowed the baler, but only the one farmer who wanted it uses it.

The baler decision shows that even with a culturally shared mindset of rejecting technological advances, decisions about technology in an Amish community are often difficult because there are real world concerns that need to be acknowledged. The set of "yeah, buts" might have to do with making a living (be cost-competitive with modern producers) or accommodating for injuries (continue a career after, say, a back injury prevents a man from doing heavy lifting).

Still, the Amish are committed to a rural lifestyle and have an appreciation for living intimately among nature and God's creation, and that devotion has led many communities to decide farming will be the last thing that technology will change, Bill explains. "They really want to hold the line against mechanized farming," he says.

In northern Michigan, some Amish communities that Bill knew were staunch about using old-fashioned hay mowers—the wheels of the mower drive the cutting blades as the mower is pulled across the field by horses. "But one problem is that the type of grasses native to northern Michigan are very hard on that type of mower," Bill says. "And in that colder climate, you just don't have as many BTU's to dry out the hay quickly." Modern equipment crushes the hay as it cuts, so the hay dries faster. Many northern Michigan Amish had problems producing enough quality hay for their cattle and horses, so they hired the work out to general society farmers who would just come in with modern equipment. But there are northern Michigan Amish farmers who still adhere to an even more primitive harvesting style. "In Gladwin, the farmers go out into the field with sickle-bar mowers and then harvest the hay with a hay fork and stack the hay loose in the barn," Bill says.

The difficult part comes when old-fashioned farming techniques become so uneconomical that young men cannot support their families and then take jobs in construction, which often requires them to hire drivers to drive them to distant job sites. In that situation, the adherence to a simpler technology erodes other important principles of Amish life. The father is no longer at home during the day, and might even be gone for overnight stays. And the father is more reliant on automobiles, even though he is not driving. And the career option is more removed from the land.

Oddly enough, for Bill and Tricia the issue of technology adoption became acute in their washing machine decision. Wringer washers are the norm in Amish households. Wringer washers have a barrel for the water and laundry, and the barrel moves back and forth (the agitation cycle), with the choice of power source dependent on what's allowed by a given community. Power possibilities include electricity from a gas or diesel generator, a belt or gear drive from a small gasoline engine, a battery charged by a solar cell or a gear driven by a horse on a treadmill.

One problem with wringer washers is that women must lift clothes soaked with water and manually feed them through the wringer to remove the water. The clothes are remarkably heavy, and Amish families often have many children—meaning much laundry. The Mosers had six children. And Tricia had health problems that limited her strength when she lifted pound after pound of wet laundry from the tub, day after day.

Bill and Tricia appealed to their church to allow them to use a different kind of washing machine. The washing machine they wanted would wash and spin the clothes like a typical modern washing machine and had been developed by an Amish man in Pennsylvania to run off of air power. The air pressure would be provided by a diesel engine driving an air compressor. "The washing machine was actually more technologically advanced than a typical washing machine," Bill says. And it was more expensive, $1,700. The Amish goal of not using electricity from the grid was achieved. The goal of providing for Tricia's health limitations was achieved. But was the spirit of a low-technology existence sustained? Does that really matter in this instance? "To be honest I became a little frustrated with the Amish fixation on this particular piece of equipment," Bill says. Later on, Bill and Tricia will take me to visit a community where I see a wringer washer propelled by a pony.

As one might expect, the more conservative Amish groups tend to reject technological change without weighing the advantages or disadvantages to a great degree, Bill says. "I can appreciate that, the non-acceptance of technology carte blanche," he says. "It does help preserve a way of life and a community; I see that."

Yet even low technology communities still make concessions to technological advancement, showing just how difficult it can be to hold the line. In the lower technology community of Gladwin, for example, "even the houses are built generally the same," Bill says. "The layouts, even the flooring, almost everybody has oak flooring."

The Gladwin homes have kerosene lamps; no propane is allowed. Also the kitchen sink has a hand pump that pumps water from a cistern, and the sink has no drain. To heat water, the family puts a bucket on a woodstove or has a water jacket on the wood-burning cookstove. But within this low-technology scene a small piece of advanced but tucked-away technology exists. Outside is a small pump house with a Honda gas-powered engine inside. The engine powers a water pump, and the water pump fills the cistern and also provides pressured water to one sink, a sink mounted just inside the back door so that people can wash their hands as they come into the house from working outdoors. Some of those decisions seem arbitrary—why pressurized water to one sink and not others? But Bill sees the decisions as more about achieving a goal of preserving a way of life than achieving a goal of blind adherence to a technology standard.

In addition to technology boundaries helping the Amish function separate from society, the boundaries also achieve another central goal of the Amish, Bill explains: the rules are intended to achieve unity through uniformity among members, help tamp down our natural human tendency to cultivate and obsess over our individuality. Help keep the congregants' thoughts and energies focused on what matters most: serving one another, serving the community, achieving a strong brotherhood and above all serving Jesus.

The boundaries on electricity seem especially vague to me, and Bill acknowledges that electricity is becoming more vexing for Amish communities as the technology for electricity evolves. Banning electricity used to be a rather simple decision. Electricity coming in from the power grid was forbidden because it was a very real connection to the broader society that the Amish are sworn to separate from. The power itself was a connection to society and all the gadgets that ran off electrical power were connections to society.

But then generators made electricity possible in a way that was separate from the power grid, and about the same time mechanized farming made it extremely difficult for Amish farmers to survive economically, and many turned to workshops to make a living. "At first, many communities allowed power tools in shops, that's where it began," Bill says. And power limited to the shop and not coming from the grid was a pretty easily managed thing; the line still stood bright: no power in the home and still no power from the grid.

But then battery technology evolved, and all sorts of tools can now be powered by battery. Complicating that, solar and wind power evolved—charge batteries that way. "So from a stewardship and responsibility standpoint, that is much more environmentally responsible than running diesel engines," Bill says. And stewardship of creation ranks high among Amish values. But the downside is advanced batteries and alternative power complicate the Amish decision tree. "With home appliances now designed to run directly off 12-volt electricity, you can see where suddenly it's not much different than living a life where power is coming in right off the grid." And a multitude of gadgets are now up for discussion. "For a lot of churches, it means 'we'd have to evaluate every device plugged into a battery,' and most churches are just not willing to do that," Bill says.

I'm curious about broader technological dilemmas, how the Amish might feel about some of the technology-inspired ethical quandaries that general society itself is grappling with. I bring up the most out-there technology dilemma I've heard of. "I read that people who have had a child die are the most ardent activists pushing for the cloning of humans—what do you think of that?" I ask.

Bill looks to the ceiling. He pauses for a while. "You see, what am I even able to do with that information?" he says. "I have no way to influence that. It does not affect my life.

"There is a passage in the Bible that says, 'do not be overly concerned with rumors of war.' And it implies do not be overly concerned with distant issues that you cannot change. Like global warming. I can send money to some far off group in Washington, and who knows if it will have any impact, or I can reduce my carbon footprint right here."

Horse, Buggy, Solar Array

Bill tells me that to better understand the how and why of living low on the technology ladder, I should meet him in Kentucky to visit two plain Christian communities: Brownsville and Caneyville. Members live even lower technologically than most Amish communities, but what makes them most interesting in Bill's mind is they have unexpected ways of deciding which technologies will be allowed and which will be banned. The main point is they don't worry so much about trying to be flawlessly consistent in the rationale of what they accept and reject. For example, if they drive horse and buggy, ban chainsaws and forbid electrical wiring in homes, is it okay to approve an advanced solar power array for one of the shops? The answer in Brownsville is yes.

Bill suggests we first stay with his friend in Brownsville to get a sense of how the lifestyle works and then head to Caneyville to talk to Bryce Geiser, a community leader who has long helped guide the low-technology vision.

I arrive on a rainy Tuesday night in mid-November, weaving my way down the Wendell H. Ford Western Kentucky Parkway and then tracing Kentucky's narrow asphalt two-lanes to Brownsville. Beyond the sweep of my wiper blades, my headlights shine on a small yellow highway sign near Brownsville that shows an Amish buggy—a reminder to drivers to be on the lookout. I can't help but consider the skinny strip of asphalt shoulder and the ditch about two feet further on. A buggy driver—say a mom with three kids in the rig—would have no choice but to stay on the road and trust a driver's awareness and reflexes.

I drive through the tiny, night-quiet town, and on my way south soon see the Peace Valley Market sign that Bill told me to look for. I turn up the road. It twists over a ridge, drops into a valley and goes to gravel. I'm in the rolling hills of central Kentucky, barely a mile from the western border of Mammoth Cave National Park. The night, capped with clouds that obliterate all light from the moon and stars, is pitch black.

I wind through the community on the gravel road. A sawmill appears in my beams—spotlighted stacks of lumber and wagons parked here and there. I drive on, and soon the gravel runs out and turns to dirt two-track. Bill, Tricia and daughter Sarah had arrived earlier, and we'd been staying in touch by cell phone. Bill said he'd be standing along the two-track to guide me to the house. I suddenly see him in the glare of headlights beside a thicket of bamboo, darkness all around. He wears the denim coat and pants that I've become accustomed to seeing him in. I see no lights to indicate a house—just Bill harshly lit-up in my high-beams in the night.

We'll be staying in the home of Jason and Edna Troyer, son and daughter-in-law of Freeman and Wilma Troyer. Freeman and Wilma are still in the process of building their home, about 20 yards from Jason's. Until it's done, they use the kitchen and living room in the basement walkout apartment of Jason's home as their main living space.

Bill and I walk the short dirt trail to the house. As we near, I see a faint glow of light through the windows. Freeman greets me inside the sliding door of the walkout. He's in his late fifties, has a friendly, round, suntanned face, longish, mostly white beard and longish hair, wears plain denim pants, leather suspenders and a work shirt. The only light in the space is a DeWalt work flashlight—the kind with a squarish rechargeable battery as a base and that stands up like a little lamp. I squint at the bright light, which quickly falls away to dim shadows.

Talking to a journalist is not a common thing for Freeman Troyer, so he's wondering about protocol, about deferring to the guest. "Did you want to get started now?" he asks.

But the long drive and the fact that by Eastern Time—my body-clock's home time zone—it's midnight, means I'm too tired. Freeman shows me to a small room with a twin bed. He gives me the flashlight in case I need to get up in the night.

Freeman and Wilma were Amish their entire lives until they moved to Peace Valley, which is technically not Amish due to some differences of scriptural interpretation; though to an outsider the lifestyle appears identical. The main reason for their move had to do with their own journey of faith, a desire on Freeman's part to interact with the outside world a little more, spread the word of Jesus and their interpretation of the Bible more broadly. "We have something good. Why not share it?" he says. That meant leaving the Pennsylvania German dialect of the traditional Amish church and going with English language services. As for the more primitive technological lifestyle required at Brownsville, that wasn't so much a draw for Freeman as it was simply part of the package that he figured he could accept.

Brownsville is an offshoot of Caneyville, which itself is an offshoot of a plain Christian community that once operated in Cookeville, Tennessee, but which is now defunct. Like Amish communities, these plain Christian communities limit the number of families in their churches. So when Caneyville—which began in 2004—grew to about twenty families, the community decided to start another community and bought 180 acres of long-dormant, bramble-tangled farmland near Brownsville, twenty miles southeast. Just a year ago, there was a single structure on this land, a small, three-sided sheet-metal outbuilding, maybe a shelter for horses or cattle. But today there are a half-dozen houses in various stages of completion, a sawmill, a produce market/meeting hall and a metal fabrication shop. We'll see the buildings when we walk around come daylight.

I wake to hear Tricia and Freeman's wife, Wilma, talking as they make breakfast, and I wander out to the living room amid the scents of coffee and baking to sit in a chair beside Bill. Behind me, stacked against the wall are boxes of Freeman's family's things, staged here until their home is completed. Freeman comes over, first sliding the DeWalt flashlight into a homemade ceiling-mounted hanger. He sits down and we chat for a few minutes about how I'd like to do the interview. At 7:05, Freeman calls the rest of those present to the living room for morning devotion. Tricia, Wilma, the Mosers' daughter Sarah and Mary—an eighteen-year-old girl from Marion who is staying with Jason's family; each woman wears a white cap and a long dress. The men—Bill, Freeman and the Troyers' teen son Joey—wear plain clothes as well.

"Johns 17, Jesus's prayer for us," Freeman says. "Bill would you please read?" and he hands the worn Bible to Bill. All bow their heads as Bill reads in the humble space: The cement floor, the cinderblock walls, the first-floor trusses visible above, the boxes stacked nearby.

"My prayer is not that you take them out of the world but that you protect them from the evil one. They are not of the world, even as I am not of it. Sanctify them by the truth; your word is truth. As you sent me into the world, I have sent them into the world. For them I sanctify myself, that they too may be truly sanctified."

The passage is a touchstone for all Amish and other Anabaptists, words that help them define boundaries for living both with and without the modern world—in the world, but not of the world.

We move to the table, set for eight and crowded with classic farm breakfast food. Scrambled eggs, toast from homemade bread, homemade jam, baked oatmeal, cranberry juice, coffee. Freeman asks Bill to say the meal prayer.

The food is hearty and feels close to the earth. The space is warm. All of which can be in part attributed to the white wood-fired cookstove/oven in the kitchen, a stove that Freeman built when he owned a small factory that made wood-fired stoves in Marion, Michigan, and sold them under the name Kitchen Queen Stove Company.

Freeman tells of a technological innovation he developed for his stove, one that turned the stove into a convection oven. He describes a small-diameter metal tube that channels air from the room through the firebox and into the oven. The super-heated air is never contaminated by wood smoke, and the air stream circulates the heat around the cooking food.

Did he patent the innovation? "No. Because all that gives you is the right to sue, and we don't litigate," he says. Freeman recalls a man who phoned him a few times wanting permission to copy Freeman's design innovation, but Freeman wouldn't agree. "I told him, why don't you just think of a better idea and make that instead?"

Freeman's best year in the wood-fired stove business was 1999. "The Y2K thing," he says. "I had so many orders, I made stoves as fast as I could, but even then I couldn't fill them all before the end of the year." And once New Year's Eve 2000 came and went, and Americans saw that, in fact, all computerized systems weren't going to crash, and that all of America would not be living like the Amish, everybody with un-delivered stoves cancelled their orders. "Some people who already had stoves asked me to buy them back," Freeman says. "I would tell them that I'm not in the business of buying stoves, but I did buy a few back for half price."

The day opens with blue sky above, and the sun is just inching above the eastern ridge when Freeman leads Bill and me out into the frosty morning for a tour. We step carefully over a one-log bridge, slick with dew, that traverses a small creek in front of the house and then walk into the farm field beyond.

Freeman stands in the open field. Behind him, the frost on the green tangle of daikon radish tops is starting to melt—the giant white radishes push down a foot or deeper and are ideal for breaking up hard soil without mechanized equipment. Around his feet, a flock of about twenty free-range chickens bustles, busily pecking at the greens and earth. Freeman tells a story from last summer. He woke around midnight, maybe later, to see the light on in the chicken building. Heading out to see what was up, he found most of his family butchering about twenty-five chickens. A dog had some-how broken into the coop and slaughtered them. The simple-living family could in no way afford to allow the meat to waste, so whoever discovered the problem rounded up a work crew in the middle of the night and they all pitched in without complaint. I recall a Bible passage oft-quoted by the Anabaptists, from Genesis, when God is explaining the new rules now that Adam and Eve are banished from Eden: "By the sweat of your face shall you eat your bread"—to feed and sustain yourselves, hard work will be required for you and all of humanity forever more.

Freeman himself is amazed at what has been accomplished at Browns-ville in one year—all without the use of power tools. "All winter long,

Caneyville would send down a van of men every work day to help," he says. They'd labor alongside the men in Brownsville to put up the homes and work buildings. No power tools meant all the boards were sawed by hand, hammered together with a grip and a bicep. This is a difference between the Amish and the Christian communities in Brownsville and Caneyville: the plain Christian communities do not use gas- or diesel-fired engines, which means no air compressors to run air-powered tools, which many Amish construction crews rely upon.

We look around the field at the results of the labor. To the southwest, a tidy house flanked by three hoop-houses stands on a low ridge. To the southeast, another tidy house, this one still wrapped in Tyvek, a small out-building nearby houses a metal fabrication shop. To the northwest stands another home; beyond our sight are the sawmill and a few more houses. We walk to the market building, also built in the last year. "We did $35,000 of business in the first year, so we were pretty happy with that," Freeman says. The market helps fund the community, but it is also a way to interact with the people of Brownsville, part of the outreach ethic that appealed to Freeman.

In the cold dormancy of November, the building is hushed, but evidence of a busy season surrounds us. Five half-gallon jars of unsold pickles on the shelves, coiled irrigation hose, a half-dozen new double-hung windows still packaged up and leaning against a wall. We walk to the workspace in back, a kind of small warehouse with a cement floor and rough-cut lumber walls and a stainless steel utility sink. I ask about the loose circle of unmatched chairs arranged in the middle of the cement floor. This workspace is also where the community gathers for church.

We head back into the chill morning. Freeman is going to show us one of the technological inconsistencies that Bill told me about. We walk through the farm fields to the metal fabrication shop. The young man who owns it is not home, but trespass is not an issue. We walk into the shop, housed in the three-sided building that was here originally. The shop is tiny and crammed with metalworking equipment, mills and lathes and an electric welder. Shiny metal shavings curl on the mill work-trays. Hoses for hydraulic fluids snake through the tight space, lit in a shadowy daylight.

Freeman explains that the electricity for the welder comes from an array of solar panels a bit farther up the hill. To see it, we follow a narrow footpath worn into the weeds. It traces up the hill, around a bend, and when it opens to a field we see the bank of solar panels, each black panel about 3 feet wide by 4 feet high and canted to catch the sun's energy. "Let's see," Freeman says. "He's got one, two, three, four…" he counts the nine solar panels out loud. On a long shelf below the panels, runs a bank of 6-volt batteries, each the size of a car battery. Freeman counts them out loud too. There's a trait I've noticed about Amish, and it is a sharing of nuts and bolts business information, the cost of raw materials, production time, selling price, and a very comfortable conversant, unit-price way of discussing these things. I suppose it's because so many families are small business owners.

"So he's got nine solar panels at, well, not sure, $175? $250? each and then thirty-nine batteries at about $70 each, so he's got about $5,000 into this," Freeman says. "The cost of solar has improved dramatically in the last couple of years. Not long ago it would have cost ten times that much for solar panels." It occurs to me that the low-technology-lifestyled Freeman Troyer knows more about solar power than 99.99 percent of Americans.

We head back toward the house, and Freeman stops for a moment along the low ridge. He surveys the farm field below, the houses beyond. "A year ago, this was all brambles this high," he says, and holds out his arm to above his head. When Freeman tells stories, they seem to naturally take on a Biblical quality, like when we stop beside a patch of farm field. "This was onions, about $50,000 of onions planted, would have been an $80,000 harvest. And they were growing beautifully. Big, round onions," he says. He holds out his hands and cups them as if holding a softball. He smiles remembering the moment. "Everybody was so excited about the onions. But then just before the harvest, it rained hard for a week straight, and 90 percent of them rotted." A fungus. The pestilence.

We walk on. We cross the creek further upstream, and at the bridge there lies, sideways to the creek bed, a big plastic culvert pipe, maybe 4 feet in diameter and 20 feet long. "One night it rained nine inches in six hours," Freeman says. The resulting flood blew out beaver dams upstream, and water gushed through the valley, washing out this culvert pipe and sweeping it downstream to jam against this bridge. Water filled the valley and came within just a few feet of the walkout basement where I slept the previous night. The deluge.

Freeman gives us a quick tour of the house he is building, a cute bungalow set just up the ridge from his son Jason's house. Here he points out a technical innovation he came up with that seems like it pushes the boundaries of the low-tech rules. At Brownsville, the community requires outhouses—can be smelly and swarming with flies, especially after a weeks-long spell of Kentucky's summertime heat and humidity. And Freeman's family is used to indoor plumbing, which is allowed in most Amish communities. Freeman built the outhouse, but then connected it by pipe to the septic tank he installed for the wash-water from his kitchen. He then ran the wash water down the same pipe the outhouse uses, which will essentially flush the outhouse. "I might have the only flush outhouse in the country," Freeman says and flashes a smile. Does Freeman's outhouse keep to the letter of the rule (yes, it is an outhouse), but defy the spirit of the rule (it is not the full, challenging outhouse experience)? Is Freeman's solution a workaround that should not be allowed? In this case, the community did not object.

We are still discussing the outhouse when we arrive back at Jason's house and I see another instance of low-tech technology. On the porch, a pony walks a treadmill that is connected by gear, clutch and drive train to a wringer washer. As the pony walks, the washer swishes back and forth, and the wringer roller turns. The process takes an hour and a half per load. Mary, the girl visiting from Marion, stands doing the laundry. Jason takes a break from hand-grinding venison sausage to explain the system he welded up himself.

As we're talking, a young woman suddenly appears on a trail that runs beside Jason's house. Behind her walk about ten children, a mix of boys and girls, the oldest about ten. The little girls all wear white caps and long dresses. The boys wear denim pants, button shirts and suspenders. The short parade is a school class going to the field to play. For me, it's a time travel moment, like suddenly it's, say, 1753 and I'm watching children from colonial America slip single file down a narrow path, hop rocks to cross a creek, and then skip on to the sunny field beyond the shadowy woods.

One downside that Freeman sees of such a low-tech approach to community life is it relies so much on physical labor that it's difficult for older people to make the transition. Would the approach effectively lock-out, say, a 60-year-old seeker couple that doesn't have the family and friends network that Freeman and Wilma have? "I'm planning to do the books and sales for my son's stove-making shop," he says. If not for that, he's not sure what he would do for a living—he doesn't think he could work hard enough, long enough and fast enough to farm in a low-tech way.

Of course, for centuries, the Amish lived technologically pretty much like everybody else, essentially up until the automobile and the electric grid. I ask Freeman about that, if technology wasn't a defining issue back in the day, why now?

"Yes, my father used to talk about back when Amish and Mennonites and non-believers worked side by side, all farming together," he says. But that was when everybody farmed small farms and many people still farmed with horses. "You know, at one time, this valley had about the same number of farms you see here now," he says, sweeping his hand to take in the land. But then he sidesteps the question. "You know, I'm not really the best person to talk to about the reasons for technology. You should talk to Bryce in Caneyville."

Caneyville and the Low-Tech Purpose

W e pack the car trunk with Moser family suitcases and bid adieu to the Troyers, who cluster where the dirt path meets the two-track. As we say good-bye, a fat pink pig, about knee-high, grunts once and stares up at us from a bamboo patch a few feet away. He's endearing, to be sure, but with winter coming on, he's got a date with the hand-cranked sausage grinder on Jason Troyer's porch.

Bill slides into the passenger seat up front, and Tricia and Sarah climb into the back. We head off on the twenty-mile drive to Caneyville—the parent community to Brownsville—to meet with Bryce Geiser, one of the community's founders.

Turning off the main highway, we edge along a narrow run of asphalt that traces the shoulder of a ridge. Where the road turns to gravel, signs of the community appear. A couple of shop buildings, small factories maybe 150 feet long and 100 feet wide, stand on the north side of the road. In one factory the community makes Pioneer Stoves, a wood-burning cookstove popular with plain people, preppers and people in Europe. The other main factory makes jams and jellies. Those businesses, plus raising produce, are the three economic engines of the community.

Across from the workshops, three carts with horses stand idle in the shade. Catching my eye is a beautiful matched pair of molasses-dark mahogany horses, their harnesses trimmed with silvery medallions about six inches apart. Set against the dark coats of the horses, the buttons emanate a muted but striking glow in Kentucky's soft November light.

Beside the horses sits a flatbed from a semi-truck packed with industrial-scale metalworking equipment that looks to be from the 1940s or 1950s. A 12-foot-long Cincinnati brand shear that can slice big metal sheet, a lathe and more. A little later we meet the thirty-something man who recently picked this all up at auction. He's Solomon Stoll, the same man who owns the solar-powered metal shop we had toured at Brownsville, and that's where this gear is going. If it's possible for a low-technology community to have an inventor, Solomon is it for these people. I learn later that he also converted a gasoline engine to run on the off-gas of burning wood.

We see no cars besides mine, and as we stand there, a young man rides past driving what Bill calls "a one-horse," a small, single-axle flatbed cart pulled by a horse. The driver stands like a chariot driver, but leans against nothing, jostling down the road, reins in hand, balanced, comfortable, but riveting and dynamic too. I turn to watch as he heads up the hill into a sunny opening framed by autumn trees. He's backlit, the dust from the cart wheels a glowing cloud. It's another beautiful time-travel moment. The authentic everydayness of the scene—not something from a re-enactment village, but a true, honest and daily act—made it seem in a startling way that the rider had just torn through the space time continuum and ridden in from another century.

We ease through the community to drop Sarah at a friend's house, and as we drive, the valley opens before us. The scene is not unlike Browns-ville, but a decade further evolved. The farm fields are neatly charted in the valley bottom. The houses, dotted here and there on ridges and rises, are completed—no Tyvek or piles of lumber to be seen. The road is well graveled and kept.

Bryce Geiser, his wife, Eloise, and two of their eight children—the others are grown and live in either Caneyville or Brownsville—live in a trim, smartly designed two-story, encompassing maybe 2,500 square feet, with a covered porch wrapping around the ground floor. Inside, the home speaks with an earthy intelligence. The first floor walls are stacked cut stone, visible both inside and out. The floors and trim and cabinets are varnished natural wood. The effect is warm, but simultaneously sleek and spare, echoing the look of some contemporary design. Point being, the words primitive or low technology would never occur to you as you take in the space.

Bryce welcomes us in. He's fifty-five, maybe 6 feet tall, lean, has a beard and glasses. He has the sensibility of a friendly, self-made intellectual, with a quick, confident and inquisitive mind and a charming ability to spin stories.

He soon tells me he dropped out of high school.

Bryce considers himself a seeker, but his background is not quite as mainstream as the Mosers, raised as they were in a middle-class suburb of Detroit during the 1960s and '70s. Bryce was raised in a conservative German Baptist home in Indiana farm country, and his family worked construction trades. Unlike Amish children, the children from his church went to public schools, including high school. "So we were basically indoctrinated with the blessings of technology and where technology has brought us, with increased lifespan and medicine and making our lives easier," Bryce says with an unmistakable irony.

He would have graduated in 1976 if he'd stayed in school, but during his sophomore year, word spread through the Conservative German Baptist churches that students could take correspondence courses at home and get a GED. "A lot of us got excited about that," he says. "You could get a job, stay out of the high school atmosphere and finish school at home. And so that's what I did."

Eloise says something to us from the kitchen, but I don't quite catch it. Bryce nods to the digital recorder. "I don't know how to shut your machine off, but she wants us to eat," he says. I reach over, push the right button, and we break for lunch.

Eloise sets out a large and varied lunch. Bryce asks Bill to say meal prayer. As everybody bows their heads in prayer, the motion of the white caps tilting down adds a subtle but evocative element to the scene. Bill thanks the Lord for helping each of us to spread the Word using our own particular talents. I suspect that in covering such ground, Bill is hoping to help Bryce get comfortable with the idea that somebody like me, who would not be considered a Christian, will be telling the story we are here to explore.

We pass food around the table, a slightly sweet cabbage salad with sautéed ground meat, a Worcestershire-flavored spaghetti dish, a fruit salad with home-canned peaches and pears, homemade jam with homemade bread. The food presents a plain richness that so clearly springs from the same place as this life and this home.

As we begin to eat, Bryce displays his irrepressible need to know. "So I'd like to turn the tables on you," he says, and looks squarely at me. "What is your faith background?" I can feel Bill and Tricia go tense beside me.

"I was baptized Catholic. We went to church off and on ... and then not at all," I say. I leave it at that and look at him. There's a pause all around the table. People are hoping for more. I'm remembering a promise I made to myself at the start of this book project, that I would never embellish or lie about my own state of Christianity in order to make the Amish or others feel more at ease with me, because I felt doing so would poison the spirit of the mission.

"So, started off Catholic, that faded away and nothing took its place," Bryce says, looking at me.

"That's pretty close to it," I say.

Bryce looks at me. Silence again hovers over the table. He's apparently processing, but also apparently wants me to know he's still okay with the interview, because he then tells a story about a Mennonite woman he has known for many years. She became a journalist with a large newspaper in Florida. She covers crime, a lot of murders, and she has left her Mennonite roots. Eloise says, "She is the kind of reporter that likes to come up with their own theory about who did a murder." The Geisers still enjoy visits with her and they remain friends.

After lunch, Bill, Bryce and I settle back into our chairs in the living room while the women clean up. I ask Bryce to tell it from the beginning, how he ended up here in this Christian community that has hewed to a technology path even lower than most Amish communities, and most importantly, explain the why.

"I got married very young. I was eighteen, I was almost nineteen, and we were just full of ambition. We were gonna show the world how to raise a family. We wanted to be domestic," Bryce says, in a tone that lightly chides his younger self for his idealism and naïveté, like saying, "We were going to change the world!"

"We young parents, we young fathers, would talk about it, and we'd say we really need to be involved in agriculture. That's the way to raise a family," he says. The family he grew up in has "scattered." His sister became mainstream Baptist and has been married three times. His brother married a Jehovah's Witness. "I wanted a very strong family. I wanted to be close with my children ... I wanted to be close with them." I can't help but recall how strong this same desire was in Bill and Tricia when they began their journey, how it shaped their own purposeful approach to life.

Bryce and his likeminded friends asked the farmers in their area how to get started farming. "They'd say, 'Just give up. It's not possible,'" Bryce says. "Unless you inherit a farm, that's a good way to do it, but other than that, it's just too hard. They'd tell us the days of our grandparents are over. You can't have a few hogs and a few cows and forty acres and make it."

Meanwhile, Bryce had to support his family, so he followed in his father's path, becoming an electrician and later branching into air conditioning and refrigeration work. But he felt that just wasn't how he wanted to raise his family, being away from his children all day and often into the night.

"Then we heard of this new thing, growing produce and selling it at a market," he says. This was the tail end of the '70s, and though they lived in the heart of Indiana farm country, almost nobody was raising and selling market produce because farmers were all growing commodity crops: thousands and thousands of acres of corn and soybeans, but very little produce to buy at market. One huge benefit to growing produce: "You could start on a dime," Bryce says. There's no need to buy, say, a herd of dairy cows and stainless steel milking equipment, and the acreage can be minuscule by corn or soybean standards, so expensive equipment like combines isn't needed. His parents sold Bryce and Eloise six acres, and the young couple cut into the soil for the first time.

"We worked very, very hard," Bryce says. "But we didn't know anything. We had no teachers. We didn't grow up Amish." That first year they made a "very teeny bit of money," but farming got in their blood. "We thought, all we had to do is grow a little bit more and work a little bit harder and this will surely work." So that winter, Bryce went back to the electrical and heating and refrigeration work. "I worked furiously so we could farm that next summer," he says. And that next summer they expanded, figuring that if they could make a teeny bit on five rows of some crop, they could make twice that with ten rows. "So we worked very, very, very hard that next summer, and we made about the same amount of money, and we thought, Well, that didn't work."

They kept at this cycle for a few years, but they could never make it self-sustaining. "We had car payments and house payments … we weren't washer- and dryer-payment people, but there was always the electrical bill to pay, the telephone bill to pay. Always these things that made it impossible to tighten our belt and survive."

Bryce and Eloise and their friends figured they needed to adjust their lives more than they had thought. They figured there was some kind of lifestyle package that could make it work economically, and they just had to discover it, put it together. And by the way, "Our church didn't support this," Bryce says. "They were just saying, 'There's another kook who's probably going to go broke after a while. He'll learn his lessons. Everybody else did.'"

Three families stuck with the mission. They talked about, planned and worked at lowering their lifestyles to the point where they could work at home, be with their children and start farming. Eventually they figured Kentucky would be the place to go because the land would be cheap. "We said, Let's go there, back in the hills. Back in the sticks where the hillbillies lived. We'll figure out how to live the life we wanted to live. We'll buy a farm. We'll all three settle on it."

But the three families immediately discovered the process, even at this intimate level, was more complicated than they'd anticipated. Right at the start they had to discuss technology. What would they accept? What would they reject? "One of the men always wanted to look at it based on what was economically feasible. I had my own ways of looking at things that made me make these other choices. The third man had ways that made him take this other path," Bryce says. He put earnest money down on a farm, but then the seller backed out. They found another farm, but disagreements were plaguing the group.

"In this mix, in this swirl, in this confusion of trying to figure it out, we ran into a man by the name of Elmo Stoll," Bryce says. Stoll was a founder of a plain Christian community in Cookeville, Tennessee, and he listened to the families' stories, heard their dreams. "And he looked at us and said, 'Oh my. There's just no way you are gonna get there. You are too confused. You need teachers. The things you are trying to do are too big.'"

Stoll was relentlessly discouraging, but his concern came from a supportive place. "He feared we were going to be like all those hippies in the '60s who left the city, went out and did their homesteading, finally realized that's a dumb thing to do and went back to Silicon Valley and got their high-tech jobs and away they went," Bryce says.

Elmo Stoll, it turned out, was very seeker-friendly, and he told Bryce and his friends to come live there for a while, and they would learn what they needed to know. Two of the families made the move. "It was one of the best decisions I ever made in my life," Bryce says.

At the Cookeville Christian community, the Geisers learned what to do and how to do it. "We discovered that yes you can lower your lifestyle to the point that it doesn't take much to live. And you don't have to earn a tremendous amount of money. And you will never get rich. And you will have a hard time paying your medical bills. And you will have a hard time buying land. But you can make it. You can tighten your belt to the point where you can make it through the winter."

In that plain Christian setting, the Geisers felt they'd found the Garden of Eden. "We were happy as larks," Bryce says. Eventually they left

Cookeville, along with one of Stoll's sons, Aaron, (his brother Solomon came later) to launch a similar community at Caneyville. The expansion has been a success, but one looming issue, Bryce says, is making the money to buy the farm for the next generation, or at least helping to buy the farm. The community will be putting a lot of thought toward that in coming years.

Of course, what's driving this lifestyle is not just a desire to live low-tech, but to fulfill the community's commitment to Christianity, to Jesus. But what does that really mean? Even with my limited knowledge of the Bible, I know that Jesus never weighs in on, say, the use of chainsaws or electric toothbrushes. How does a low-tech lifestyle achieve a closer bond with Jesus?

"A very important point is that in making these decisions, these decisions about how we are going to live and what we think is best for our church and community, we are not trying to make decisions about what God approves of and what God disapproves of," Bryce says. "We are not trying to say, 'This is right, and this is wrong.' We are not saying, 'Jeff, you came in a car, so you are wrong.'"

So what are they trying to do? "We are trying to ask, 'What is the wisest thing, for this group of families in Caneyville, Kentucky, how is the wisest way for them to live? What would further our ambitions, our goals, things we are trying to accomplish? We are always trying to answer this question: If Jesus were here, what kind of a life would he want us to live? We realize we haven't arrived at the perfect answer, and it may be that this church over here has arrived at a better answer, or that church over there, but we are just trying to answer questions for Caneyville, Kentucky, not for the rest of the world."

Technological
Consistency

The guiding principle contained in the question that Bryce presented, "How would Jesus want the people in this community to live?" seemed to me essentially the same as the principle that Bill explained when I asked him what guided technology decisions, and the answer might be something like "work hard, but above all, do so in a way that makes time to spend with family, makes time to spend studying and sharing faith and makes time to build community."

Bill had brought me to Caneyville to gain a more nuanced understanding of how those broad, guiding principles played out in daily life, in daily technology, how they determined what was allowed and what was forbidden.

In assessing technology, what's in, what's out, Bryce openly concedes that the need to make a living plays a big role. "I think you'd find that across the board—Amish, Mennonites, everywhere. They are looking at, What do we need to maintain our lifestyle?" So, maybe electricity is not allowed in homes, but it's allowed in a shop because electricity might be needed to make some particular product cost-effectively. Or you find in many Amish communities that phones are not allowed in homes, but phones are allowed in shops because they are so important to the flow of business. Although, in Caneyville, there is only one phone in the community, and the businesses and the members share it. Most of the business happens by mail.

But in some other important ways, a two-tier technology standard clearly exists in Caneyville—things are allowed in the shops but not elsewhere. And making a living is what drove the technology decisions. "We were thinking, you know, produce farming is a good way to raise a family and earn a living, but there are families that that doesn't really fit, and we need to have shops," Bryce says.

Having shops meant needing some kind of power supply. The community first considered "a horsepower." That's the literal term for connecting horses to a carousel and having them walk around and around, turning a shaft that then turns gears or belts. "But horsepower tends to be very troublesome," Bryce says. "We had a six-horsepower for the woodshop, and you get six horses out there, they'll break just about anything. There's a tremendous amount of torque on a horsepower."

The woodshop horsepower broke down frequently, so the community knew it needed something different, and they decided on a wood-fired steam generator. Why the community allowed wood-fired steam engines instead of gas-fired is something of a mystery, Bryce concedes. "I think the only explanation is that we didn't like the exploitation of the earth that petroleum involves," he says. But also, a wood-fired steam engine sidestepped the slippery slope that people foresaw with allowing a gas-fired generator. "We said, well, if you allow gas engines, you have the lawn mowers, and you've got the rototillers, and you've got the string trimmers. You can run anything with a gas engine. But with a steam engine all you can do is run a shop ... well, you could run a car, but nobody does. So the steam engine is not going to impact our homestead lives. It is only going to impact the financial future of the community."

I ask Bryce if he can recall a technology decision that was particularly contentious, something that might have even led to people leaving the community.

The divisive technology: the bicycle. The issue didn't arise in Caneyville, but at Cookeville, in the early days of the community. "It was contentious enough that two people left the community," Bryce says. Most people saw the bicycle as a tool they wanted. "We dreamed in our early, youthful enthusiasm that it would replace a lot of our need for the automobile, and we started using it that way." Cookeville members would ride bikes everywhere, even heading out on trips of fifty, sixty, eighty miles to visit or do business of one type or another.

"Yeah, they were kind of legendary," Bill affirms. His comment reminds me again of the communication flow within the plain-person world. Somehow, Bill, when living in northern Michigan back in the late '90s, knew that the people of Cookeville, Tennessee, were riding their bikes on long trips.

"I know that seems strange to you that the bicycle would even be a question," Bryce says to me. "But a lot of Amish communities and the Scottsville Mennonites [a large conservative Mennonite community in Tennessee] have forbidden them. The reason is it gives a lot more mobility to the young people. They can very quickly find themselves in town and back home again with a bicycle."

But in this realm of making decisions about faith and technology and life, it's difficult to sort out exactly how the final decisions get made for each individual. So, for example, what exactly was it about accepting the bicycle that led the two people to leave Cookeville? Bryce shrugs, says he doesn't really know. The people might have viewed allowing bicycles as a slippery slope situation. Channeling their thoughts, he says, "Oh, I see. We are leaving the old faith. This is not the way our fathers have always done it, and we can't accept this. This is worldly, modern, who knows where we are going from here."

Sometimes, Bryce says, a community makes technology decisions based simply on the fact that some members don't want some particular thing, even if they can't articulate a compelling argument. "They just have a gut feeling, and you don't want to run over them, so you end up with a very inconsistent package," he says.

Based on what I've observed of the Moser family and in visiting with their friends, I have come to believe that consistency in technology limitations is not really possible, in part because it seems the slope can be slippery both ways. That is, if every decision about technology is considered a precedent based only on its technological aspects, then nearly any relaxation of technology limits could be used as a basis to dramatically expand all limits. (e.g., if we allow the electricity in a headlamp, then we have to allow electrical wiring in the home). And likewise, if technology is rejected only on the basis of technology aspects, then that precedent, it seems, could be used to argue the community back to the Stone Age (e.g., if we ban the light from headlamps, shouldn't we ban all lights?). I explain my observations to Bryce and Bill.

But it turns out that in the Conservative German Baptist culture in which Bryce grew up, attempting to maintain consistency in setting technology boundaries was a very big goal. Until Bryce moved to Cookeville, it never entered his mind that being inconsistent was even an option for plain Christian living. In his German Baptist Church, "we were always trying to find some way to make it work [to have consistent rationale in technology policy], and especially we did not want to make a church rule against something that could be lawfully used." Lawfully, that is, from a scriptural standpoint. The German Baptist church of Bryce's youth felt that "most modern technology could be used in a lawful way, in some beneficial way," Bryce says.

Bill weighs in on this idea too; clearly he has given the concept of consistent technological rationale a good deal of thought. "That is a big thing, do we have the right to limit this if there is no prohibition against it in scripture? You could make the case that scripture doesn't speak on it, so why not."

One of the very biggest inconsistencies Bryce's childhood German Baptist church worried about was forbidding the ownership of a technology, but not forbidding the hiring of that technology. So, the most obvious example would be the Amish practice of forbidding the owning and operating of cars but allowing the hiring of drivers. In Bryce's childhood church, maintaining consistency meant people could own cars. But when he moved to Cookeville, Bryce had to adopt the practice of hiring drivers. He recalled a conversation with Elmo Stoll in which he implored Stoll to at least allow the community to buy a single van. It would save a lot of money—hiring drivers is expensive—and it would be more convenient.

Elmo said, "Bryce, it's like this. I don't have a problem with drinking a soda pop once in a while. But I do not want a soda pop machine in my living room, because I would drink too much and my children would drink too much, and we'd just consume way too much of that stuff, and that's why I don't have a car out in my parking lot." So, the decision about technology stepped away from the narrow argument of consistency and was based more on broader lifestyle goals.

Today, many plain communities are running into a similar inconsistency with the Internet. Community members might view the Internet as something necessary to economic survival or simply as offering something convenient—easy mail ordering of hard to find buggy parts or farm equipment, easy sharing of news. But the community members may not want to fully adopt the Internet. "Many of us were sitting back and saying, So, are you [the Amish] going to hire that out?" Bryce says. At some level he appears to enjoy watching others grapple with the same tech issues he does. "And sure enough, that's what some are doing. They are hiring people to respond to email or even do Internet searches."

As Bryce tells me this, I recall when I chatted with the Mosers soon after they'd become Amish, and Tricia told me about the journalist in Montana who had shot a photo essay about Amish children playing baseball at a church where the eldest Moser son, Tristan, was teaching. When Tricia told me, "You can see it on the Internet," I naturally thought, You use the Internet? And I recalled the Moser boys telling me they could get really good clearance deals on outdoor clothing on the Cabela's Bargain Basement website. The Mosers' Amish Michigan community would not have allowed home computers and Internet, so the Mosers just went to the library and surfed the Internet there.

These things left me puzzled from a consistency standpoint—can't use light bulbs, but can use the Internet?

So the need to make a living can lead to technological inconsistencies. The need to respect community members' personal opinions, their guts, can lead to technological inconsistencies. The desire to respect longtime cultural practices leads to inconsistencies. Even the need to come down on one side or another of a scriptural debate can lead to inconsistencies. "Long ago, we decided not to be consistent." Bryce says, of the Caneyville community. "Like you say, even if you try to make everything consistent, in some way you are messing up somewhere, you are being inconsistent in another way." As he recalls it, the decision to be okay with inconsistency evolved in the early days of Cookeville, not so much through policy discussions at community meetings, but more through ongoing talks as community members worked side-by-side building the new community. "While you were out cutting sorghum, you were talking about, Well, how are we going to be consistent? It was never a formal decision, it was just a conclusion that basically all of us came to. We will have to let that kind of consistency go in order to attain another kind of consistency."

Bill brings up an issue that's woven into the idea of consistency: technologies that essentially duplicate the technology of general society while ostensibly adhering to the letter of a community's low-tech law. So, for example, not having electrical wires provide power in a home, but using a gas-powered electrical generator to charge high-tech lithium batteries to run bright LED lights in the home. "We in Amish circles pretty much duplicated all technology," Bill says with a sense of resignation. And he acknowledges that he and his wife participated in the trend. They purchased a $1,700 clothes washer that was powered by an air compressor in the shop. "It has air switches, it agitates, it spins, everything is air powered," he says. "Really, it didn't feel that much different than when we were living on the grid."

Bryce listens and nods his head in a knowing way. "Yeah, I don't want to get to that point," he says. "It's just an expensive way to accomplish the same way, the same standard of living." But laundry, he concedes is a vexing issue for low-technology people because it's physically difficult and unrelenting work—especially given the large families many plain people have. The Caneyville community had to evolve to a laundry solution. Working with classic wringer washers "takes either a strong older girl or a dad," Bryce says. Early on, the community was encouraging dads to pitch in with the laundry. "But after a while, Dad gets tired of that and thinks there are other things he should be doing," Bryce says.

The original laundry alternative was people built horse treadmills to drive their washing machines. But treadmills for full size horses are expensive to build, and a horse is expensive, so the horse treadmill was basically a $3,000 motor to run the wringer washer. Eventually people realized a pony treadmill was better. "Pony treadmills were pretty cheap, and you could get a worthless pony for $50, and the more worthless the better. If he's a little bit wild and not very tamed, you just put him in there and let him go." Most people now use the pony models, which is what I'd seen earlier in the day at Jason Troyer's house in Brownsville.

I'm wondering if, by openly acknowledging a willingness to be inconsistent, if that sidesteps a lot of debate, dials down the emotions and arguments.

"You need to understand that we are a relatively new community. We've been here nine years, and even the whole Christian community movement is only twenty years old, so we are dealing with people who have made the choice to be here, people who said, 'We like your package. I want to come and live like you are.'" The everyday seeker from general American society just accepts the rules, is looking forward to living in that plain and novel way.

I remember Bill calling that fresh seeker verve—that desire to live as low-tech as possible—as "trying to out-Amish the Amish." That is an entirely different situation from what Amish congregations are dealing with, in Bryce's view. He thinks that because Amish people are born into a low-tech existence, and are coming from generations of that life, they are less likely to romanticize low tech. "We actually find that people from an Amish background find it harder to understand why we have the technology limits we have," he says.

When Bryce and his family first moved to Cookeville, he thought the low-technology life there mimicked how Amish people lived. So he was shocked when Amish people would visit and "they'd laugh at us and say, 'You live so low, why do you do this?'" One of the most common complaints centers on the outhouse. "I think maybe Bill and Tricia even mentioned that when they visited here," Bryce says. He looks at Bill and smiles a wry smile.

Bill gives a somewhat sheepish nod. I recall Freeman Troyer's flushing outhouse modification, which I'd seen earlier that day.

"This probably isn't fair," Bryce says, "but it seems like the Amish are just geared to say, Why can't I have more?"

Is there a technology that lives forever on the fringe, on the ragged edge, never fully embraced, never formally accepted, but never quite rejected either? Bryce pauses for a moment and his eyes look to the ceiling as he considers Caneyville's landscape of low-tech rules. "Well, okay, one area that often comes up, since we don't allow gas engines, there is one machine that is very, very practical and much speedier, and it also accomplishes a lot of things that we would like to promote, and that is called a chainsaw," he says. A lone man can cut a lot of firewood for his family, bank it for winter and save a lot of time and possibly money if the alternative is to purchase it. "We often run into this question, 'My dad is coming for the weekend and he's wondering if he can bring his chainsaw and maybe cut a little wood for me.' We tend to look the other way," Bryce says.

I admit I had expected him to conclude with, "and so we let our families have chainsaws." But no, that boundary still runs clear and bright.

I'm curious if something like health would play into a technology decision. For example, what about electric toothbrushes? They are proven to be meaningfully more effective than non-electric toothbrushes in preventing gum disease, and gum disease is proving to be considerably more damaging to overall health than previously thought. Would an electric toothbrush— tiny electric motor and all—be okay?

Bryce goes quiet again as he contemplates the question. "Well, I could imagine that it could be accepted if there was a very clear cause and effect, and especially if it was something bigger than just dental disease. You know, if you would just do this, none of your people would have heart disease, we'd be very interested in that technology."

Bryce goes quiet again as he thinks about it more. I can feel his mind working through the discussions, arguments, rules that have occupied his mind for decades and that have led the community to where it is today on the tech scene. First, he acknowledges that, as with the chainsaw, there'd probably be some wiggle room. "If it was a battery-powered toothbrush, which most of them are, and you just started using it, probably nobody would say very much about it," he says. He pauses again. "Although if you were to bring it up to the community, people would say, 'Aww, let's don't get started. It's a gateway.'"

Convincing Bryce himself would not be easy. He, along with Aaron Stoll, was, after all, one of the principal shapers and keepers of the community's low-technology vision—a chief advocate of the outhouse. That role came in part because he'd lived in Cookeville and nearly duplicated its rules to form the foundation of Caneyville. "We didn't want to start at the beginning and re-decide everything we'd already decided in Cookeville," he says.

Today, nearly a decade into Caneyville's run, Bryce remains solidly on the side of when in doubt, say no to technology expansion. "If you look at what technology has actually done in the lifespan of the Western culture, we've got it up to, what, mid-70s? And the lifespans of the plain people, people living quiet, decent, basically healthy lives with exercise and diet, their lifespans aren't much different. I'm not overly impressed that you could spend billions of dollars and arrive at two or three more years average lifespan."

Is there anything currently under debate on the technology front? "No, I think we are in the mode of, Okay, we have made enough changes for a while. We've accepted enough little things here and there, we just need to give it some time. We are in a place where we can all make a living fairly easily. We don't really need technology change in order to survive in our economic climate. There's nothing we really need. In another ten or twenty years, we'll look around and see if there's something else we should be doing."

We thank Bryce and Eloise for their hospitality and their thoughts and drive to pick up Sarah from her friend's house before heading off. We ease along the gravel road and crest a little ridge. I look to the left, and I see a girl of maybe nine years old riding a pony around a carousel, not a play carousel, but a work carousel—a "horse power" in the parlance of Caneyville. The girl and pony are providing power to something. She of course wears a white cap and long dress and just seems relaxed into the job at hand. Then Bill says, "Look, a boy chasing a pig!"

And sure enough, about 50 yards behind the girl we see a boy of about the same age waving a stick and running after a pig. The boy wears plain denim pants rolled up to the knee, a billowy button up shirt and suspenders. He's fluid and beautiful running through the field chasing the pig. I say it's a Pieter Bruegel painting come to life—the girl in long dress and cap on the horse power, the boy chasing the pig, the autumn golds in the fields and sense of harvest all around. Bill and Tricia laugh. "It is!" says Tricia.

Pennsylvania
German
and the Unraveling

D espite finding so many things right about the Old Order Amish ways and cherishing so many aspects of their Marion community, the Mosers, after fifteen years—five years in Ovid and ten years in Marion—left the horse-and-buggy lifestyle. In some ways, the seed of what eventually led the Mosers to leave was planted at the very beginning of the family's path, when in early discussions with Joni Mast, Bill's sawmill-owner friend from Gladwin, Michigan, Bill learned that Amish services are spoken in the dialect of Pennsylvania German. When Bill received that news, he was crestfallen and figured there would have to be another path, because he and his family were not likely to be able to grow spiritually when listening to a language they could not understand. After all, the journey they were on was a journey of faith not culture, and as seekers, the thing they sought most was a nuanced understanding of their faith.

What kept the Mosers heading down the Amish path is they learned that in Ovid, the community held six services a month in English: each Tuesday evening service was in English, and every other Sunday the service was in English. During German services, the church also provided translators for the Mosers, one for Bill and the boys and one for Tricia and daughter Sarah, since men and women sit on separate sides of the room during services.

When the Ovid church disbanded, the Mosers moved to the Old Order Amish community of Marion, in part because the church agreed to services in English every other week and also agreed to provide translators for the German services. The way translation worked in Marion is Bill would sit in the second to last row in the room and behind him would sit a translator, generally a young man, who would speak quietly—just above a whisper—close to Bill's ear. The services are so long, three hours, that a second translator would take over at some point in the service.

When Bill and Tricia first became Amish, they were committed to learning Pennsylvania German. But they found that Pennsylvania German is not a written language, and there were essentially no instructional materials published [since that time a Pennsylvania German dictionary and some instructional materials have been published]. What's more, the amount of time they spent interacting with their German-speaking neighbors was not enough for them to immerse and learn the tongue. Besides, they were able to get by just fine for the most part because whenever the Mosers were with community members, the Amish spoke English.

Eventually, Bill and Tricia came to see it as unlikely that they'd ever learn German fluently. Bill could understand some small bits here and there, but Tricia just couldn't get it. The Moser children, however, being immersed in school and play time with German-speaking children, picked up the language. Tristan eventually became one of Bill's main translators during church.

One of Bill and Tricia's deepest hopes was to see an Amish community established that functioned primarily in English and welcomed seekers like their family. The Mosers had visited just such a community in Maine several times, and they had friends there. Though the church was in Maine, it was officially part of the Michigan Amish Fellowship, a relationship formed after the Amish Michigan Fellowship agreed to help the community through a difficult period in the early 2000s. English-speaking Amish communities exist in North America, but they are "nearly unheard of," Bill says.

But overall, Bill and Tricia were grateful for the accommodations the community had made for their lack of German fluency and immersed in community life. "We had no desire to make the church change, do something it didn't want to do," Bill says.

Bill and Tricia understood why in the Amish community, having an English-speaking family in the congregation caused concern among some members. A pillar principle of the Amish faith is to function separate from general society. The uniform clothing the Amish wear erects a dike against the flood of mass culture. Driving a horse and buggy erects a dike. But the greatest protection, the greatest barrier between Amish and general society is speaking a language that has essentially no instructional tools. The Amish consider these barriers central to the survival of faith, culture and community. And when an English-speaking family with two adults and six children drops into an Amish church with maybe thirty families, the foreign language barrier, the thickest, tallest, stoutest dike of all, begins to leak a little bit.

Bill and Tricia respected that concern and saw that process, that leakage, in action. In an Amish community, many children do not learn English and are not exposed much to English until they begin school. "But when my kids were little, and we'd go visit with a family, that family's children are being exposed to English at an earlier age," Bill says. The Mosers' children played in English, and Bill and Tricia would be conversing in English with parents.

For some people, that introduction of English to the home was an uncomfortable interaction, and it brought slippery-slope kinds of questions: If we allow English-speaking for our young children, will they be more likely to want to be part of general society when they are older?

Bill recalls a conversation that happened maybe five years after the family moved to Marion. It was after a church service, and there was a small group of men sitting and talking, and the topic of language came up. One younger man said, "If somebody wanted to marry somebody who knew only English, the German would go away, you would lose the language," he said. The implication: If you lose the language, you lose the entire future of Amish nation.

As the conversation progressed, Bill posed a situation to the men. Let's say a person would desire what the Amish church has to offer, but spiritually the person feels he's not getting fed to the fullest because he doesn't understand all of what's being taught. Is it right to condemn that person to a lesser church because of language standards? The man advocating for adherence to German language said, "that's a choice that person would have to make."

There was another aspect of speaking Pennsylvania German that Bill and Tricia could never get settled with. They feel that Jesus made clear that followers should spread His word, share the Bible's message with the world.

But, of course, it's essentially impossible to share the word when the word is delivered in an incomprehensible language.

As the years moved on, the Mosers started to sense a shift in their community, a subtle but growing uneasiness over the presence of English language in church and community. Bill feels that a good portion of the resistance emerged from events that transpired in the nearby Evart Amish community. The Evart church had been relatively open to seeker families coming in from general American society. But suddenly there were a half-dozen seeker families attending the church and wanting to officially be baptized into the congregation. While the church leadership officially continued to welcome the seekers, many of the church members grew concerned about a weakening of their cultural fabric. The seekers felt a growing chill.

Some good friends of the Mosers who were among the Evart seekers decided to leave the church and moved to a Mennonite church in Kentucky—Mennonites and Amish share the same broad statement of faith. Bill understands the dilemma and even the reaction of the Evart community. Imagine a small community devoted to a strict preservation of practices and language having to help six families transition into a different culture, helping them learn all the things the Mosers had had to learn: how to make money, how to drive a horse, how to plant a garden, how to sew clothes, how to can a year's worth of food, how to learn Pennsylvania German. The process takes one-to-one service.

After seeing what transpired with their friends, Bill and Tricia couldn't help but wonder what it might mean for them. They had been in Marion for about six years at this point. "I asked our ministers, do people in Marion feel the same way that the people in Evart feel? The response I got was, 'We don't feel that way.' I thought they meant 'we the entire church.' But looking back on it, I think they really meant 'we the ministers.'"

For years, as the Mosers had listened to translators during church and never felt fully assimilated because they couldn't speak the native tongue, Bill and Tricia's quiet hope for an English-preaching Amish community kept them going. Seeing the example of the Maine congregation, nearly entirely English-preaching and a part of the Michigan Fellowship, gave them plenty of reason to sustain that hope.

But as time progressed, Bill and Tricia came to sense that there was more discomfort with the English language in the broader Michigan fellowship than they'd previously perceived. To the couple, that meant their hope of an English-preaching Amish community, supported by the Michigan Amish churches, was pretty much extinguished. "When we found out that there are some strong attitudes against that, attitudes that would prevent that from ever happening, that kind of took the wind out of our sails," Bill says.

The Mosers rejected one option that might seem obvious: Move to live with the Amish congregation in Maine. "We thought about that a lot," Bill says. "But we were concerned that over time, if they stayed with the Michigan fellowship, the Maine church would be pressured to accept more and more German, and then we'd be right back to where we are." A certain tension already existed over the use of English in the Maine congregation, leaving the Mosers wondering where the pendulum would eventually swing.

Eventually the Mosers decided to join an Amish Mennonite church in Missouri. They would be driving cars again. The services would be in English. They announced the decision in December 2012 and planned to move in the coming June.

The
Wedding

J ust a few weeks prior to leaving the Amish in Marion, the Mosers hosted a wedding at their home for a young Amish couple whom they cherish.

The wedding had been scheduled for several months, so despite the Mosers' deciding to leave the church, the wedding plans moved forward. The day was understandably one of deep and conflicting emotions for the Mosers: at the very moment when the family was poised to leave the community, every man, woman and child they had grown close to or had had disagreements with in the past ten years was gathered at their home. Naturally the Mosers wanted the day to be a celebratory one, and they were devoted to keeping the conflicted parts of their emotions in check.

An Amish wedding has a spirit of joy within it, Bill explains, but outwardly, during the ceremony, there is no overt celebration, and as with other church services, the service happens in the everyday spaces where the Amish hold church. "The actual wedding ceremony is about five minutes at the end of a typical three-hour church service," Bill says. One aspect of an Amish wedding that the Mosers always enjoyed is the large number of teens and young children who attend, thanks to the large families that Amish have and the inclusive nature of the culture. It would be unheard of for an Amish wedding couple to say no children are allowed at their wedding.

For the Mosers, hosting the wedding meant clearing out the pole barn where they had built pallets for their home-based business. Measuring 40 by 64 feet, the building was one of few in the community large enough to hold 450 invited guests—375 of whom attended—so practicality was also part of the reason the Mosers were hosting.

Amish communities have something called a bench wagon that transports benches and other things, like drinking glasses, plates and silverware needed for church services and the lunch following. The benches are in fact plain benches: 8-, 10-, and 12-foot-long planks with no backs. The Marion bench wagon is enclosed, with a roof and steel barn siding; the wagon has a hitch that can be towed by horse or truck. Because church services are held at people's homes, the bench wagon goes to whichever home is hosting service on a particular Sunday, and a few people arrive to help set up a day ahead of time.

With 450 people invited to the wedding, though, the Marion church had to call in bench wagons from three other church districts to have enough seating. "Some people were out a few days before the wedding measuring the building and figuring out the best way to arrange the benches to fit everybody," Bill says.

For the Mosers, the emotional charge of the wedding was amplified by the wedding couple's story and their connections to the Moser family. The groom was a young widower with a three-year-old boy. The Mosers had known him and his first wife as a couple. They had celebrated the birth of the couple's son. They had grieved with the young father during the loss of his wife and helped him along as he struggled to regain his footing after his wife passed away. His child was cared for by another Amish family as he worked his way back to emotional health. When he was ready for a new relationship, the groom came to the Mosers and asked them if they would express his interest to the woman who would eventually become his bride. The Mosers were something of surrogate parents for him.

"Among our churches, dating is very purposeful," Bill says. "People only date with the intent of getting married." If a man feels God is leading him to a certain woman, he conveys that message through an intermediary, which is usually the young lady's father. The couple dates, but quickly ends things if it appears God's will does not support the union. "Marriages are not arranged or anything like that," Bill says. "It's just that it's a very purposeful process. There was no casual dating in our church."

With the groom hailing from Ontario and the bride coming from a large Amish community in Illinois, there were many out-of-town guests who had hired drivers to transport them to the wedding. "Sometimes you will even see a big bus, like a Greyhound bus, pull up and a bunch of Amish get out," Bill says.

Amish weddings typically happen on Thursday mornings, although this was on a Wednesday, and it started at 8:30 a.m. Being, for the most part, a normal church service with a brief marriage ceremony at the end, the service proceeded in typical fashion. The group sang ancient religious songs in German for about 45 minutes. Then a minister spoke for another 45 minutes. Then another minister read from the Bible and spoke for half an hour. Then the bishop spoke and prayed and then performed the brief wedding ceremony.

In accordance with Amish custom, six chairs are placed directly in front of the ministers and the wedding couple sits beside each other in the two middle chairs. Their witnesses sit on either side of them. When the time for the wedding ceremony arrives, the bishop calls the couple to the front of the gathering.

"The actual marriage ceremony is pretty low key," Bill says. "The couple stands up. They say their vows. The minister puts their hands together and blesses them and prays with them. They take their hands away and return to their seats." There is no kissing or other showing of affection. But despite the prevailing sobriety, "you can tell there is an undercurrent of joy," Bill says.

For Bill, the most conflicted emotional moments came after the ceremony ended and before the meal began at their neighbor's house a quarter mile down the road. He watched as the hundreds of guests left his family's pole barn. The people were dressed in Sunday Amish style. The men in black pants, white shirts, vests and hats. The older men wearing black jackets. The women and girls in dark-toned prairie dresses—called cape dresses—with white caps. Bill stayed behind, wanting to make sure the house was empty and closed up properly before heading down to the reception.

And in that time, standing at the window alone in his house, watching the men and women walk in small, intimate clusters down the road, he couldn't help but contemplate the power of community, the power of faith community in particular. He couldn't help but troll through images in his mind of similar scenes he'd witnessed out that same window during the past ten years. The Amish children on their way to school, walking or running, on horseback, on bikes, driving buggies, hanging on to the backs of sleighs and sliding down the snow-covered road. The many Sundays watching families in buggies driving past on the way to church. He stood there considering all the reasons why he and Tricia had worked so hard to find a community of shared faith, and why he and his family were now leaving this particular version of community.

Admonishment

B ill and Tricia knew that joining a community of faith with strict rules for living meant they were also signing on to a system that enforced those rules. That is, they knew that if they broke the rules, they would be admonished in some way. They would be subject to sanctions. In part, this idea of accountability was an aspect of faith that they specifically sought. They were looking for a community of faith that had high standards for behavior, a community that applied consequences when members did not adhere to agreed-upon standards that were based on a shared interpretation of scripture.

But even in a society where rules are remarkably precise, where rules govern such minutiae as the design of a woman's head cap, there is judgment and nuance involved in deciding where a rule should be enforced and how a punishment will be applied. And Bill concedes he did not always agree with where those enforcement lines were drawn.

When I ask Bill to give me an example of how, in a society where the rules seem so clear, a situation can still be murky. He offers a simple case. "Let's say the gas motor on a family's wringer washer breaks down, but the electric motor is still attached and works, so they hook up an electric generator to it until the gas motor can be fixed," Bill says. Many Amish communities would accept that use of electricity as a temporary fix, with the understanding that the family would be having the gas motor repaired soon. "But what if the family isn't getting around to having the gas motor repaired? And what if the reason is they can't really afford it at the time?" Bill says. How strictly should church leadership enforce the rule? After all, the family needs clean clothes.

When the Mosers first joined the Amish faith and lived in the Ovid community, the leadership there had a relatively relaxed approach to enforcing rules. "For Tricia and me, following the rules was pretty seamless," Bill says. "In part it was the newness of it all, our enthusiasm and wanting to make that change." But also leadership did not address every little violation or transgression; they only took action if a member repeatedly did something against the church's ordnung—the document that spells out the community's rules for living. "They kind of gave each member their space—that's not quite the right concept, but it was something like that," Bill says.

When the Mosers moved to the Amish community in Marion, they joined a community where rules are more strictly enforced, but even then Bill says it wasn't difficult to live within the rules of the Amish. "It's not constantly on your mind. You are not always thinking, Is this in the standard or isn't it?" he says.

Discipline did, however, come to bear on the Mosers when, after ten years in the Marion community, they announced their decision to move to an Amish-Mennonite church in Missouri and leave behind the church they had belonged to for a decade. A key point of conflict was the Mosers' joining a church that allows members to drive cars. For Bill and Tricia, the decision to get around by horse and buggy had always been more about showing solidarity with their community of faith; they accepted horses and buggies simply as part of the lifestyle package, but they never really viewed driving horses and buggies as part of a scriptural command or a fulfillment of Jesus's wishes for the world.

Tricia recalls when they first joined the Amish, somebody was telling her of a family that left the horse-and-buggy Amish and "joined a car church." "Something about the way the woman said it made me think, There's something wrong with that?" Tricia, says. But also, at first Tricia was so unaware of Amish feelings about driving cars that she didn't even know what the person meant. "I first wondered if she meant those churches where people drive up and stay in their cars, like at a drive-in movie," she says.

Even though the Mosers would continue driving a horse and buggy until they left Marion six months after they announced their move, the church decided that the family would no longer be allowed to share communion with church members. The Mosers were not shunned, that is, church members were still free to share meals and visit with the family, but by not being allowed to share communion, Bill and Tricia were relieved of their church responsibilities and were not involved in church decisions, though they were still considered members of the church.

As the Mosers understood the rationale of sanctions surrounding their leaving the Marion community, church leaders were concerned that other members of the church would become enamored with the Mosers' example and join a church that allowed car driving and allowed a broader interaction with general society, including spiritual activities like outreach and mission work.

Relative to driving a car, the couple understood how important the horse-and-buggy way is to preserving a cohesive Amish community, but they felt that driving horse and buggy is adhering to an important cultural norm, not adhering to a biblical principle. The Bible never weighs in on mode of transportation, so why should it be subject to religious sanction?

"If a person believes in the horse-and-buggy way, they should be strong enough to not be tempted by others driving cars," Bill says. "And if it's a young person who is tempted, then the father of that person should have the young person's heart enough to talk about those issues and help the young person to not be enticed on that issue."

Still today the Mosers don't fully understand how the decision to not allow them to participate in communion came about. They were not at the meeting where the decision happened, and at the time the church did not have a resident bishop, so they aren't sure who was involved in deciding. They only found out about their changed status when their neighbor, one of the church leaders, told Bill about it when they were out in the forest collecting sap for maple syrup.

Looking back on the evolution of events now, the Mosers are able to view their Amish church's decisions with understanding. They see that church leaders were grappling with a situation that, justifiably or not, caused leaders to worry about foundational elements of their Amish community—if the Mosers' decision inspired a bunch of members to drive cars, the community could disband. But at the time, the Moser family felt very conflicted and could not understand why they were not allowed to share communion, because, after all, they were moving to a church that shared the same Anabaptist principles of faith and they would be driving horses until they left.

It's not possible to be curious about the Amish without being curious about the practice of shunning—a formal curtailing of communication with an individual because of a transgression, a violation of a church rule. Like so many other aspects of Amish culture, the specifics of shunning—how it's implemented, transgressions for which it's implemented—vary significantly among the hundreds of Amish communities dotted around the Americas and the globe.

And even within a specific church, the notion of shunning is a nuanced thing. Shunning is part of the continuum of enforcement tools that a church uses to encourage members to adhere to rules of the community. Shunning would be the most extreme measure and would generally be accompanied by ex-communicating the member from the church. In some Amish churches, the shunning and ex-communication would involve a termination of communication with a member, even between family members. But in other Amish churches, shunning and ex-communication would mean the individual, though officially removed from the congregation, could still attend church. The shunned individual could not share meals with friends and family, but otherwise could communicate at will. For example, a shunned member could be visiting family, and when dinner time arrived, the shunned member would eat in the living room while the rest of the family would eat in the dining room; after dinner, visiting would resume.

Prior to taking the extreme measure of shunning a church member, the leadership would typically hold private conversations with the errant member to convince him or her to change. A milder version of shunning, called avoidance, is also an option. Avoidance would allow limited contact with an individual, like, say, once a week. For example: Your brother has left the church and is now driving a car, so he is not allowed to visit friends or family in the church more than once a week. When a shunned church member repents his sin and shows genuine commitment to returning to the ways of the church, he or she is generally forgiven and welcomed back in a formal ceremony of repentance.

Feelings of belonging or not belonging, feelings of acceptance or rejection—these are powerful emotions that are fundamental to our emotional well-being. Measures such as ex-communication, shunning and its milder form, avoidance, are overt and calculated efforts to leverage those potent emotions to convince people to stay in the fold. Proponents of shunning—which Anabaptists believe is a biblical dictate—say it is designed to draw church members back to the community, to create a longing so the person rejoins the body of Christ. Opponents say shunning is too damaging psychologically and emotionally and should be stopped.

Shunning goes back to the very foundation of the Amish faith. Jacob Amman, originally a Mennonite, strongly advocated for a more strict implementation of shunning, and when Mennonite leaders refused, Amman instructed his followers to split from the Mennonites in 1693, and the Amish came into being.

Bill and Tricia have always appreciated the Amish culture's willingness to forgive, so they have questioned at times how that squares with the Amish practice of shunning when members change churches, especially if a person is keeping the same statement of faith in a new church. After all, religious tolerance is a foundation of Anabaptist belief, as is a belief that church membership should be entirely voluntary. Few, if any, Christian sects have suffered as much as the Anabaptists have because of their refusal to be coerced into a specific religious belief—it's that very refusal to be coerced that caused other Christians to kill the Anabaptists. "We are nonresistant, but nonresistance goes deeper than just not pulling the trigger on a gun," Bill says. "It also means not trying to dominate or rule somebody's conscience with guilt and coercion."

Bill and Tricia believe that people should share their faith and give reasons for the hope that lies within them. "But we shouldn't coerce or force them in a guilt-driven way," Bill says. "People who are devoted to their faith are susceptible to that—myself included—we want to hold our children, our church members, to a way of life, to that specific expression of Christianity, and that is where things can get mighty sticky."

The Auction

On the last Saturday in April, under a flawless blue sky and the surging sunshine of spring, a few hundred people gather for an auction at a farm not far from the Mosers' home in Marion. By 10:30 a.m., the auction has begun, but still more people are tracing the back roads in cars, in horse-drawn buggies and on bicycles to converge at the big sale. A mile or so from the farm, I pass a single-file line of eight Amish boys on bicycles, pedaling hard in homemade denim pants, suspenders, wind-billowed shirts and wool caps. I pass a carriage driven by a man and carrying three women, their white caps brilliant inside the black canopy of the buggy. I pass other buggies, other bikes, all clearly on their way to the springtime auction made up of two families' belongings, including those of the Mosers'.

At the auction entrance, I see Matthew Moser directing traffic, and he tells me to pull ahead to a hay field in the distance. I drive slowly along a line of buggies and horses that stretches as long as a football field. The horses are all tied to a pasture fence with carriages and trailers parked nearby. All carriages are black, some are clean, flawless, shiny, others are splashed with mud. Many have the bright orange slow-vehicle triangle on the back, some do not. Working trailers are mixed in—one flatbed has a car seat bolted at the front for the driver.

For the Mosers, this is of course a bittersweet day. They are auctioning off the things they will not need in their new car-driving life in Missouri, and each item sold is another small reminder that their time in the Old Order Amish life—fifteen years—is not ending as they'd hoped it would. Both families selling their belongings today are leaving the Old Order Amish.

"Forty-five, 45, 45, forty-fiiiiiiiiiiiiiiiiive!" A dramatic pause ... "Sold! For 42 and a half." The voice of an auctioneer, amplified through a speaker, drifts across the fields—the grasses still a short, stubby mix of barely green and winter brown—and into the leafless forest beyond. With two families' worth of things to sell, the auction has to move quickly, and two callers sell simultaneously. The fact that each seller family also runs a small business means equipment is a big part of the offerings. From the Mosers alone there are several commercial grade woodworking tools: routers, a drill press, table saws, sanders. The other family ran a bakery, so commercial grade ovens, cooling racks and display cases have drawn people with small-business dreams of their own. Farm equipment is lined up in a field to the west.

Yoder Auction runs the sale today, and Leroy Yoder himself is one of the callers. A man in the crowd tells me Yoder recently won the title of State Champion Auction Caller. He wears a black brimmed hat, blue button-up shirt, suspenders, has a trimmed beard and sits in something that looks like a cotton-candy-vendor trailer, like you'd see at a fairgrounds, mounted in the bed of a pickup truck. It inches among the items. Moving in tandem is a man who steps among the merchandise and holds up things that are being auctioned at the moment.

Microphone in hand, Yoder never stops calling. The man among the goods picks an egg box from a stack and holds it high. "Must be a bunch of people here who have eggs!" Yoder cajoles into the mic. And the auctioning begins.

About two-thirds of the people here are dressed plain, the other third are a mix of everyday northern Michiganders. One man's T-shirt reads, "Put camo on anything and it gets better."

"Sold, to buyer 268!" Yoder yells.

I wander down to the scrum of men and women gathered to follow the auctioneer. It seems that for many people, the day's primary purpose is to just chat and reconnect after a long winter. In an outbuilding, Amish women in blue dresses and white caps sell cookies and pie—pecan, blueberry, cherry—in thick slices for $1.50. The smell and smoke of grilling bratwurst and hamburgers wafts through the air. On a trampoline, a half-dozen girls aged maybe four to nine, also wearing blue traditional Amish dresses and white caps, bounce up and down in the April sun.

I find Bill standing among the crowd. He has a sense of anxiousness. He's talking to me, but is distracted. He keeps cocking his head, looking off, listening to the prices that things are going for. He's monitoring the vibe of the buyers. Are they in a spending mood? He is selling a career's worth of equipment—what will it bring? What will the day's take mean for his family's new life? He watches as the caller stops at a pile of maple sap tubing—thin tubes that convey maple sap from a tree to a collection container—that the Mosers are selling. The family had just begun maple syruping a couple of winters prior, and it had become a meaningful part of their income and a treasured activity in their lives. It will be no more.

"There's Joni. I'll Introduce you," Bill says. It's something of an ironic moment. Joni Mast is the man whom Bill credits for first connecting him deeply with the Amish nearly twenty years ago, and now he's here bidding on the Mosers' belongings as they prepare to leave the Old Order Amish ways. Joni wears a black felt hat, classic denim pants, a dark green shirt. He raises his hand to bid on the maple sap lines. A boy of about 5 hugs his leg, rubbing the denim near Joni's calf between his fingers.

Some of the Mosers' things speak clearly of their Amish lifestyle—horse halters, for example "Hardware's in good shape!" Yoder calls to the crowd. But much of the family's possessions are what you'd find in any American garage where a family has five boys and a girl. Four pairs of bright green and blue swim fins go for $7.50, a black garbage bag filled with basketballs goes for $20, a hunting bow, a coiled orange hose, a fishing net, a snow shovel, rusty bike wheels, K2 downhill skis. "The boys bought the skis cheap at second-hand shops. They'd tie a rope to a horse and ski down the road, up and down the snow banks, like water skiing," Bill says.

"Now there's a bargain! Give me ten and go!" the caller says, starting up another item.

Tricia walks up to talk with us and watches as the man holds up a box of household things. "That's a 'sad iron.' You heat it on the stove. A lot of women would have two so one is always hot," she says. Then the man holds up another box. "Hey, that's our wedding stuff," she says, and laughs. For all her sensitivity and intuition, Tricia has a striking ability to live in the moment and not dwell on sentimentality. She's looking ahead.

Bill cocks his head again, hearing something. "They're selling your washing machine," he says.

"Oh, I gotta see this!" Tricia says, and hurries off through the crowd to the other caller. Bill explains it is a traditional wringer washer with an electric motor that they ran off a generator. It goes for $360.

"Bailing twine here!" Yoder calls. "With all the rain this spring and a little sunshine, should be a good first cutting!"

Bill stands at the edge of a trailer of items. He's shoulder to shoulder with a mix of plain men and regular American guys, but he's also, at this moment, alone with his thoughts, listening, watching, contemplating the days ahead. The sun shines through the open weave of his hat brim, casting a mottled shadow on his face. He wears a denim jacket, loose-fitting homemade denim pants. His arms are crossed. Dirt from the dusty April field patinas his shoes.

"Deal of the day right here!" Yoder calls. "A swing set still in the box, all the hardware!" It goes for $20.

Bill keeps a vague running tally of prices in his head. A moment of disappointment comes when selling $3,000 worth of galvanized blower pipe. "Can I get started with $100?" Yoder calls. A man bids, but no bidding momentum builds and the price quickly stalls. The tubing goes for $300. You can feel a soft silence around Bill as he takes in the low price.

Occasionally Yoder asks Bill a question about an item. Something electrical goes up. "Bill, you said it's a 210 not a 110, right?" Bill quickly steps up from the crowd, he has a bemused look on his face "220" he emphasizes—there's no such thing as 210 electrical. It's a lighthearted moment—electricity not so much an Amish thing.

By 3 o'clock, all of the Moser items except the farm equipment have sold, and the auctioneer has moved on to the commercial bakery items. The farm equipment will be sold at the end of the day.

Bill feels the family did well except for the blower pipe. He won't really know until he sees the numbers. He stops to talk with a friend named Freeman Troyer. He had been the bishop at Marion but had recently left, moving with his family to a plain-living but non-Amish community in Kentucky. One reason for his move was a desire to do more outreach, convey the Anabaptist interpretation of Jesus's teachings beyond the Amish community.

Meanwhile, the auctioneers' voices still lay down the day's soundtrack. "Commercial oven! $2,000! We got a new shooter on board! We're playing with bigger marbles now!"

I go into a tent and buy a pecan pie. Bill introduces me to the woman selling it. When we step back into the sun, he explains that she and her family recently moved here from an Old Colony Mennonite community in Mexico. They were granted U.S. access for religious reasons, but still did not have permanent status and are unable to visit their family in Mexico. As Bill explains it, the Mexican family felt that their community had become too inward-looking and too removed from the Bible, that the colony life had become simply a set of cultural rules to be preserved, unmoored from Jesus's teachings. They wanted to find a more faith-rooted community, but could not find one in Mexico, so they moved to be with the Amish church in Marion, Michigan.

The story of the family from Mexico is another reminder that the Amish defy the stereotypes general American society has of them—simple people fixed forever in place and time. There is a part of Amish history and culture that tells of a surprising mobility when the Amish are faced with aspects of religious persecution. The family from Mexico comes from a group that originally moved from Western Europe to the Ukraine in the 1800s at the invitation of the czarina as she sought farmers to tame a difficult land, and they sought religious freedom. Then, as the Bolshevik Revolution gained force, the Mennonite colonies—thousands of people—feared anti-religious sentiments and moved to Canada in the early 1900s. But then in the 1930s, when Canada required families to send children to public school, the Mennonite colonies leased trains, put their essential possessions in boxcars and rode the rails to Mexico, where they've been ever since.

With the pursuit of a life of faith foremost on their minds, they left behind the homes they'd built, the farms they'd nurtured for three decades. I suspect that before that community loaded the train, they too had a big auction to trim their belongings, and that people came from miles around to an event tinged with both heartbreak and hope.

As Bill tells me this, it seems to me that, with transition and relocation dominating his thoughts today, he can't help but be drawn to tales such as these—Freeman Troyer's transition, the Mexican family's transition, their search for the community of faith that was right for them.

By late afternoon, the only items remaining are pieces of farm equipment in the western field. The blue sky has stayed blue. The warm temperature has stayed warm. Spring's first glorious day does not disappoint. Apparently indulging in the moment, a young Amish man drives a trotter horse attached to a sulky—a two-wheel harness-racing cart—up and down a line of pickup trucks in a field. The auctioneer's pickup drives slowly to the farm equipment, and a cluster of men and boys walks behind. Soon, Yoder's voice starts up again. The cadence flows across the big swoop of valley field, echoes back off the leafless trees.

"We got a barrel for hog water! Who'll give me 10?! ...7.50?! 7.50?! ... seven and a half! ... now 10! now 15! ..."

Thinking back on the day, Bill recalls the conflicted feelings one would expect he'd have. "We really liked Marion. We liked the church. As far as leaving the people that we had been a part of, that was pretty difficult. But at the same time some of the people I was most connected with in heart and mind were also leaving, and a few of them were going to the same place we were going, so that made it easier," he says.

On auction day, Bill's feelings became most conflicted when watching things being sold that related to the horse-and-buggy lifestyle, because in the context of their daily lives, "that is the big thing," Bill says. Seeing the horse gear sold, it naturally brought the question to his mind: Are we doing the right thing?

"The horse and buggy ... it is a means of transportation, a way to get from point A to point B, but in our society it means so much more than that. But does it mean that for God?" Bill asks. During the auction, more than one friend of Bill's admonished him for leaving the Old Order Amish ways and cautioned him about the slippery slope of moving to a lifestyle that is higher on the technology scale and more a part of general society. Of course, Bill and Tricia had wondered about that a thousand times, and so, at the auction, each time one of their horse halters sold or a horse wagon, those questions re-emerged.

"There is always this underlying thing, that you are just going back, returning to electricity and the automobile and that you will lose the things that you hold important by being a part of what you came out of. A couple of people who I really respect and had become close to admonished me along those lines very directly during the auction that day," Bill says. He didn't agree with the depth of spiritual peril that his friends saw, but he was able to appreciate the sentiment. "They gave a warning in love," he says.

"I believe we should live purposefully and take the teachings of the Bible to heart and make application of them," he says. "When scripture says to not be taken up with things of the world, it's not saying those things are necessarily evil, but do they keep us entangled in part of something we'd rather not be a part of?"

Bill has a photograph from the auction day. Somebody took the photo at the auction's end. The image shows Tricia sitting in the Mosers' carriage, the horses hitched. Bill is standing. They are talking, waiting to review auction paperwork, and behind them is the auction company trailer door, with the auction company name displayed. "For me, this picture summed everything up ... with the auction sign in the background. It was a day tinged with regret, even though we had the anticipation of moving on to something that we felt would be better for us."

But the Mosers were convinced that it was God's will for them, and that conviction led them along. "Without that aspect, feeling that God was leading us, it would have been extremely hard, and without knowing it was God's will it wouldn't have been necessary to leave," Bill says.

The Good
Times

W hen Bill thinks back on the whole experience of living the Amish life for fifteen years and considers the high points, the moments, big or small, when it just felt right, a set of random images float to the top.

Since finding a community of faith was central to the Mosers' seeking, it's no surprise that Bill recalls moments when sense of community was especially vivid, and often that involved doing some kind of shared physical labor with people in his church. "Doing hay," Bill says. "That was definitely a highlight." When the Mosers lived in Ovid, where they first joined the Amish, Bill would gather up his three oldest boys—at the time ranging in age from about six to twelve—and meet a few other men and their boys at a hay field. The men and boys would work the day in the field, and along the way, they'd talk about their faith. "It was a good way to get to know them—work bees, coming together, helping someone," Bill says. "Those were the times when I bonded most with the men."

For Bill, these moments of coming together and the discussions he had were as affirming as moments in church, because conversations in the hay fields went beyond superficial chat of daily life. The men discussed scripture and big issues of life, and in that setting, connected so directly to earth and creation and God, those conversations seemed deeply steeped in the richness of faith and embodied so clearly Jesus's instructions to lead a simple life.

Bill found a similar richness of community when his family and friends would gather to hand-harvest corn. "We grew about ten acres of open-pollinated corn, planted it and picked it by hand," he says. Among his happiest memories are times of gathering the youth in the community for picking, and hauling a wagon hitched to two small horses, just tossing the corn into the wagon. "We'd put it in the corn crib and feed it to the horses all winter. It was just very rewarding," he says.

But even when Bill did hay by himself in his own fields, there was something about the process that affirmed for him the path he and Tricia had chosen to follow. "When you are raking hay, you have time to think,"

Bill says. When using literal horse power, there was no sound of a diesel engine to disturb his thoughts. "I would use the two smaller horses, the ones I felt comfortable with, and I'd just be out in the field with the horses and the hay and the whirring sound of the machinery, and I would just contemplate what I was doing and what more I would want to be doing. At that pace, without the noise and clamor of a motor, it was right," he says.

Bill also finds potent memories when he reflects back on young people gathered in his home and singing Christian hymns. Typically on the Sunday evenings following traditional church service, young people would gather to sing. As the Moser children moved into their teen years, and with the three oldest boys relatively close in age, it was common for the youth to end up at the Mosers' home for singing. "The singing with the youth and with the other families, that was definitely among the happiest times," he says.

In song there must be unity. There must be harmony. For Bill and Tricia, singing was a literal representation of ideal community—people working together in a common goal, in unity, in harmony. "What that was a symbol of, that represented all of our desires for the broader community, that we could be together like that, in harmonious relationships," Bill says. The singing also set the stage for the evening conversation as well, and in between songs, the Moser family and friends talked of what Bill calls "real things—more serious issues and less casual conversation."

It helped that eldest son Tristan became especially taken by music when he was about twelve. He studied four-part harmony and learned to read music and passed his interest along to all of his younger siblings.

It's easy to see why Bill would find such richness in seeing people from his community gathering in his family's home and forming a choir, right there in the living room, and singing praise to God. But there was even more to the experience than that. The gatherings were where Bill and Tricia and their family formed individual bonds with community members, bonds that lasted for years, bonds that will likely endure their entire lives. As the young people grew into adulthood, got married and had children, the Mosers found that some of their closest friends were not all that much older than their own children. "Those friendships were a real blessing," Bill says. "And it all evolved from our home being open to youth gathering here to sing."

I ask Bill to pick one moment from his Amish years, one small, distilled moment, when it came to him that the couple made the right decision, when it all felt really good. Maybe not a big high-profile moment, but one of those subtle, passing moments of everydayness when the realization struck.

"When we first moved to Marion, we had bought our place, but we had to fix up the house before we could move in, so we were renting two miles away. Our shop was here, and our hay was here, but our animals were at the rental place. It was a chore, bringing the hay to the house by horse and wagon all the time.

"And one night when the work day was done, we were going home with some hay, and it was zero degrees, and the boys were snuggled in for warmth, I remember saying to the boys, 'You could be living in Novi or Livonia [suburbs of Detroit] and driving to a mall or a drugstore, but instead you are driving down this road, and you have a purpose for doing it. Not just a hobby or an event or recreation, but a purpose that is actually part of your life. Do you know how blessed you are for that?'"

Three Moser
Children
Reflect

I wondered how the Moser children felt about living an Amish life. Tristan was twelve when the family made the transition—what was that like for him? Other children were too young to contemplate the change when it happened. Sarah was only four; Jacob was a newborn. Still, their broader family was made up entirely of general society people, and the children lived with that juxtaposition during all family visits. I asked three of the children—Tristan, Sarah and Matthew—to share thoughts, feelings and recollections about their Amish years. Below is an edited transcript of their interviews.

Tristan

"I was twelve when we became Amish. Of the early memories of living Amish, probably the most vivid thing was the change in transportation. We got rid of our van, and we started hitching up the horse to the wagon. And we biked a fair amount, which was new to me. In Detroit we would have biked down our block, but when we moved to Ovid, we would bike three, four, five miles to get places. So you had more independence as a twelve-year-old.

For me, the change was definitely exciting. I don't remember feeling overwhelmed or anything. At the time we made the change, we had been living in the Thumb area of Michigan, and I didn't really have any close friends there. But when we moved to Ovid, there were a bunch of boys my age and all of them were friendly, and I welcomed that. We had been visiting Amish for a couple of years, and I probably did think that those boys had a fun life, that it was an adventure being in the country.

When we moved to Marion, I was a little older, and I remember feeling more trepidation, worried about trying to fit in. Language was probably on my mind. In Ovid we didn't experience so much of a language barrier because there was a mix of a Swiss dialect and a German dialect spoken there, and they have a hard time understanding one another, so they often chose to speak in English. But in Marion there was a lot more German spoken, so I tried really hard to listen and asked friends questions, and they were really good at helping me catch on. They could tell if I didn't understand something and would say it in English.

When my cousins would visit from Detroit, I did some comparison, I guess, but more comparing that we were living in a rural setting and they were living in a suburb and that I wouldn't want to live in the suburbs, but I enjoyed visiting them. I didn't really think much about comparing the Amish part because, well, we were just living out our beliefs.

I started teaching when I was twenty-one, and the first year I taught I was in Mission Valley, Montana. It's one of the most beautiful places in the West. A friend of mine was asked to teach out there, and they asked him if he knew of anybody that could help him, and he thought of me. It felt kind of adventurous, and I was open and welcome to a change, to a kind of adventure.

Teaching in an Amish community is considered something of a service, so the pay is not high. When I started they paid me $1,500 a month, but they also provided my room and board. The first year there I lived with a family in an extra bedroom. I had breakfast and supper with them, and the school families took turns packing my lunch. It was always more than enough—I could never get it all eaten.

I got into the Amish teaching thing barely knowing how to do it. I could have used a little more training, but that is something Amish communities are not really big on. You learn as you go. So for a while there in the beginning I had a bit of a rowdy classroom, and my co-teacher and some of the church members stepped in and helped me, encouraged me to have a little more discipline, tell the children what is expected of them and enforce that. But I loved the classroom, watching the light come on in their eyes when they got something. I still do.

One memory I have from Montana is elk hunting with the boys in the church. One year we took three horses and had the gear on them. And we used them to pack the elk out. We went nine miles, just winding back into the mountains. It was just gorgeous, early, mid-September. Watching elk is something I really enjoy. They can run straight up a steep hillside just like we can run on level ground, and the bulls do it while carrying these huge racks on their heads.

So, yes, I received good support out there, teaching when I was still young, but [the importance of that support] really never crossed my mind until I'd see people who did not have that. I'd travel by Amtrak and bus and I'd see people ... I could see there was an emptiness in their lives. Something was missing. Whether it was God or even just the love of friends, people around them to care for them. A lot of people seemed to be alone in the world.

It made me grateful to have that community. There are some aspects of community life that seem kind of chafing, restrictive, but the benefits ... I was definitely aware of the benefits."

Today Tristan is married and is part owner of a steel-fabricating shop in Missouri.

Sarah Moser

"I was four when we moved to Ovid and first became Amish. I don't remember thinking we were doing anything weird because at that age you don't question things like that. But I also don't remember thinking it was cool. It was just what we were doing. I do remember my dad's old purple pickup truck, though. Now that was cool.

When I was younger, and up to the time I was twelve or thirteen, I couldn't understand German, couldn't speak it or understand it, and that was hard. And I'd be with children who would speak it in front of me, and I wouldn't understand that. And I'd think, Why am I putting myself through this?

And then when I was with my cousins from general society, I also felt a difference. I probably struggled with that more than my brothers did. Maybe part of that feeling of difference had to do with being a girl and having a long dress and a cap. Versus the boys ... boys wore shirts and pants universally, so there's less visible difference. Now I've accepted who I am. I'm more confident in myself and can understand that I have these convictions for myself, more so than it's just what we have always done, or this is what my parents did. I am friends with my cousins, and when I'm with them I don't feel like such an oddball anymore.

When I got to be a certain age, I remember thinking, we are different than our family. Not when we were at home, but when we went away and were with other people who were not plain. I'd think, Why are we doing this? Not like, Do I want to be doing this, or Do I want to leave, but more like, some people might think we are really weird. I don't think we are weird, but I might have questioned why.

I enjoy visiting Caneyville (the low-technology plain community in Kentucky) and have quite a few good friends there, and I really like their community life and how they are all set up so close together. I can go there and visit for a week or two and do the whole wood cookstove and outhouse and all of that, but I would have a hard time living that way for the rest of my life. I guess I'm a little more for a practical lifestyle.

When I was younger, I took for granted the richness of community life in Marion and how not everybody has that. I guess I took it for granted. That was just the way life was. When I got older, I realized that in general society it is not like that, and even in some plain churches it is not like that. To me, the community orientation is an important factor. To know your brothers and sisters in Christ in a community basis. And I am grateful for that in Marion, and that is one of the things I really like about Caneyville.

In Marion we lived along what people called The Amish Mile, or Amish Avenue. Almost everybody living in that one-mile stretch was Amish, maybe a dozen families, and we lived right in the middle of it. And people stopped in often. If they were going anyplace, they were pretty much going past our house. And people would just drop by because they were going past, and they'd visit for a few minutes and be on their way. And we could do that too, just drop by, drop something off, whatever. We had a cow and sold milk and cream, and people would stop by for that, too.

One thing I liked about being Amish is we all worked at home. That's not true of all Amish lifestyles, but it was how our family was. We were always right there. The boys were right there. And my mom and I were both in the house. My mom and I would do canning, and I definitely enjoyed that, and I enjoyed making maple syrup. I thought it was neat making pizza sauce in 40-quart batches. I enjoyed working in large quantities like that. That is still a part of our life that I enjoy.

When we were Amish, I didn't drive horses that much, only when I had to take my mom somewhere. Otherwise I biked. I biked a lot. And I always enjoyed biking. I don't do much biking here in Missouri because there's traffic and not much shoulder. I really miss biking. I'd bike with my brothers or with my girlfriends. Sometimes on a tandem.

As for things I might miss from the Old Order lifestyle, I'd say biking. Definitely biking. And of course I miss my friends from Marion. One thing I really liked was making maple syrup. It was majorly intense and sometimes you wanted to tear your hair out, but we miss it. We used horses, and it felt really neat using horses to gather sap. We made maple syrup with another family, had many great times together and we made the work fun.

One thing I don't miss is having to use a driver. You can have good quality time in the car. If you go somewhere and when you leave you want to talk about what happened and stuff ... if you have a driver along you just didn't talk about it."

Today, Sarah teaches at a Mennonite school in Idaho.

Matthew

"I was three when my family became Amish. I don't really remember ever thinking about the difference between our life and our cousins' lives. I don't really remember thinking, We are driving a buggy and this is different or weird. It was just what we did. I do remember our cousins coming out to our farm and thinking it was cool that we have a farm, and I remember thinking, Well, this is us, the way of our world.

If anything, I remember thinking we were better off because we could hunt and trap right around us and ride horses. We might talk about the differences with our cousins more now, but back then we just accepted each other.

I guess one big difference is my cousins are still going to school, and I don't feel like I'm missing out on much by not going to school. Now I'm working at the lumberyard and learning from the guy who is doing the job that I am going to do.

A happy memory I have from when we were in Marion was riding horses. When we drove somewhere for supper, my family would go in the buggy, but my mode of transportation was horseback. I really enjoyed that. I started that pretty young, when I had a pony, and then a bigger horse. It was faster on the horse than in the buggy. I'd just go on the roads, or if there was a two-track I could use, I would do that. I would almost have to say you have to grow up with a horse for it to be natural. Kind of like learning a language. It's easier to do it when you are younger.

In the winter we would ski behind the horse. You'd tie a rope to the saddle, and it would pull you. Somebody told us about it and we had to try it. You could ski from one ditch to the other. I was probably twelve or something. It was a big thing, actually. Some of the kids would do it behind the buggy on their way to school.

We were just like any other kids, and that's why we could still identify with our cousins, cause we were all kids. And they would talk about downhill skiing and stuff, so it's not like they never had fun or anything. But it's just ...

I'm not sure I have ever played a video game, but I have watched movies. I just never expected that we would have a TV. I wouldn't say we were jealous or anything. It was just something we knew Mom and Dad would never allow in the house, and that's the way it was.

A few things I really liked about growing up Amish. One would be me and my friends were close. We saw each other a lot. We did a lot of things together. You could see them almost every day, and being in a close community, you knew them so well. And I guess another would be the whole outdoor life thing. If we had become Mennonite instead of Amish, we would not have been so involved in horses, and I'm glad we were, that we used horses a lot. And the safety of the community was a good thing. We could go a couple miles down the road and not even think about it. Even when we were young, we could go a long way from home."

Matthew, when he turns twenty-one, will become a partner in the family's lumberyard. He still loves horses, and hunting and trapping remain important parts of his life.

Advice from Alfred and Martha Gingerich

One of Bill's and Tricia's most powerful and enduring memories, one that fueled their desire to adopt the Amish lifestyle, happened during the first visit to the farm of Alfred and Martha Gingerich, elders in the Amish church in Manton, Michigan. When the Mosers arrived that day, the Gingerich family was in the barn milking cows. At the time, the Gingeriches did not use mechanized milking, so they were milking by hand in the quiet of the barn. The sound of milk streaming into metal pails is tattooed into Bill's memory of the day, as is the sweet, rich smell of hay and corn silage in the barn. Occasionally one of the parents or children would start up a hymn, and the others would join in, the barn filling with songs of faith. For Bill, the scene was nearly a dream incarnate, a living representation of the kind of future he had envisioned for his family.

As the Mosers continued on the path to becoming Amish they visited Manton several times and spent overnights there with their friends the Kuhn family. They met with the Gingeriches occasionally as part of those visits, asking for advice from the respected couple.

When the Mosers eventually became Amish, living first in Ovid, about a hundred miles southeast of the Gingeriches, and then in Marion, just twenty-five miles southeast, they developed an even deeper respect for the family and learned that Alfred's reputation as a wise bishop reached far. When a newer Amish community in Maine was struggling, leaders there contacted Alfred and asked him to come out to help the community regain its footing. Bill was impressed that Alfred kept his advice strongly based in faith, but applied creativity and understanding and avoided inflexible dogma. Bill feels that Alfred's advice (a few other bishops were also involved) was central to the community being able to hang together and move ahead.

The Mosers are not the first, nor the last, seekers to travel to Alfred and Martha's farm to talk with them about transitioning from general society to Amish. I too drove there to learn what Alfred and Martha tell seekers. Do they caution? Do they encourage? What are the biggest challenges they see for those crossing over?

As I pull into the Gingerich driveway on a sunny, late-October day, it's easy for me to see why Bill and Tricia became enthralled with this setting and the life it represents. The farm sits on a ridge delivering a dramatic view of a broad valley and rolling hills to the west. On this day, at this moment, the valley forest glows with late afternoon sun and autumn colors—yellows, burnt reds, browns, green of interspersed conifers. The Gingerich home is classic white and perfectly kept. The barn is classic red and likewise kept. Cows stand and lie in the field beside the circle driveway. In the yard, coppery pine needles blanket the ground beneath a broad white pine.

Martha and Alfred invite me in to their living room. They are not accustomed to talking to journalists, so they convey a polite wariness. I sit in a chair by a big window, houseplants on either side of me. They sit in rocking chairs. Of course they wear classic Amish attire: Martha in black socks, blue dress, white cap; Alfred with a white beard, green work shirt, black leather suspenders and denim pants. Behind the couple, the room opens to the kitchen and its creamy pink cabinets.

Alfred, can you tell me a little about yourself, about your own faith history?

Alfred: I was born and raised Amish, and then I was away for a few years. But I chose to come back. I was in general society during those years, working at a hospital.

Why did you leave your Amish ways?

Alfred: I would classify it as just a desire to follow my own desires and follow the world. I was nineteen, twenty at the time. In that setting I was seeing girls, and I met Martha, my wife-to-be. I had been taught that there is no such thing as a happy home unless both husband and wife are Christian, and that brought me back. I repented of my sin, turned to Jesus for salvation and upon that I applied for membership in the Amish church and was received through baptism after a period of instruction, about three or four months. That was in central Ohio, in Perry County, Ohio.

How did you end up here?

Alfred: We had friends who moved to northern Michigan, and we were led to move with them. We've been in northern Michigan since 1983, at first close to Leroy for ten years and then here in 1993. We enjoy northern Michigan, but as we get older, we are not so fond of winter any more.

What do you remember about first meeting Bill and Tricia?

Alfred: Well, we've known them for about twenty years. My initial impressions, well, I was impressed with their family. They had maybe five children at the time and they were modestly attired. Not dressed as Amish per se.

Martha: They were very interesting people and they showed interest in us, in our way of life. Tricia did not have a covered head yet at that time.

Do you recall what you told them about becoming Amish?

Alfred: Anyone who is seeking the Lord and seeking to live according to sound doctrine and live according to scripture needs to be encouraged. We would encourage … and yet, on the other hand, our goal is to say, "This is what we are. This is what we believe. This is what we do." Ultimately it is their choice. And most of those type of people, if not all, find some difficult hurdles, because the cultures are so different, the Amish way of life versus general society.

How so?

Alfred: I would want to look at every person who comes asking questions, if they are genuinely interested, I would want to look at each one as a potential candidate for the kingdom of God and work from that basis. That would be my desire. And yet, experience would tell me they need to be cautioned. Have you really counted the cost of what it is to be a disciple of the Lord Jesus Christ? And especially if you should choose to serve him through the Amish church or a plain setting.

Are there certain things in particular that you caution about?

Alfred: We talk about the language. Half of the services are in German, and translation is provided for all that are unable to understand. But likely the biggest thing is that American society is very much into individualism, self-identity, versus our way of understanding scripture, which is brotherhood. We don't put a lot of emphasis on the individual. I want that to be understood, though. God loves each individual, and each individual is precious in his sight, yet when it comes to brotherhood and living together as a community, we find that people coming from general society do better if they are not there to preserve their independent ways of thinking.

In my observation, those types of people, seekers, are already getting away from television, and they are not interested in the Internet, and they need to take a real strong stand against society. They are kind of black sheep in general society. Society is geared one way: television and now the Internet give guidance to general society and general society falls in line with what those types of media are saying. So the seekers are black sheep already. They are strong-willed, independent thinkers, and their strength in society might become their weakness if they come to us. They need to lose that drive.

I see, so they come seeking brotherhood, but may not fully realize what that means for conformity and loss of individuality.

Alfred: Yes. They come to us and want to be a part, want to receive the benefits. And yet they might choose to retain their way of doing things differently. They might want to try to retrain us. And that is not all bad. In one sense of the word we are all seekers, and we may need to be retrained at times. I think it's good for the church to have those types of people amongst us, knocking on our doors at times. We tend to become wrapped up in our society, in our little world.

How often do people like Bill and Tricia come to your door and ask for guidance?

Alfred: Well, it comes and goes. Sometimes more. Sometimes less. We had a girl from the [surrounding] community coming for a year or so. She spent some time in our home, a girl from Manton. And we corresponded by mail. And in her last mail she said she is choosing to go to college instead of our way. That may change again.

Are you wary or weary of seekers?

Alfred: I wouldn't classify myself as wary. I would say caution. And weary? I have been. I don't want to be. [He laughs.] "Let us not be weary in well-doing, for in due season we shall reap if we faint not." Galatians 6:9. We can become weary of shepherding our own people at times. Those who are born and raised Amish, we have that same nature, to become independent, to become selfish, the self-identity thing. I don't want to give the impression that all the people in general society suffer that and that that's how they are, and we don't have to deal with that in our society, because we do. It's just that where they grow up in larger families, where they attend our schools, where they grow up in our communities, that strong independency tends to be curbed.

Well, it makes sense that, growing up in brotherhood and strong community you would see more clearly the benefits, rather than seeing just a loss of independence.

Alfred: Well, we had a funeral this summer. It was our son-in-law. He was forty-one years old. He died in the water, dry drowning. And he had a family of eight children. He was our oldest daughter's husband. What took place around that funeral—and we see it all the time around funerals, and passings, but we experienced it more personally with his passing—the beauty of community and the beauty of being part of a brotherhood, the help that flows. That is not only in Amish community, but it is almost like a guarantee in our community. And not just the local families, but neighboring churches, too, how they contributed, showed sympathy, and contributed food. And of course we have many local people, general society people, helping too.

Martha: Oh yes.

Alfred: But just what takes place over the time of a death and the funeral, it just feels so right to be part of a community. How would you word it, Mom?

Martha: Everybody is just there to help. They just go on with the work and just do it.

Alfred: And since his passing, and since the funeral, our daughter is the recipient of all types of benevolence, all types of gifts, money, food and offers of help. Of course, that doesn't replace her husband in any way, and yet, "bear one another's burdens and so fulfill the law of Christ." Galatians 6:2.

Any final words of advice for seekers?

Alfred: Again I say count the cost. Then put your whole heart into it. If you have just one foot in the community, it won't work. I would advise to visit quite often before deciding. Learn to know the people, and let the people learn to know them. Some people see us through rose-tinted glasses. It's best to be among the people who come well informed.

Settling into a
Broader America

F ive months have passed since the Mosers left their home in Marion, Michigan, and moved to Salem, Missouri, a rural community amid the Ozarks one-hundred miles southwest of St. Louis. The landscape is vaguely similar to that of Marion—low hills unfurling in an easy, elongated roll, small farms, pasture interspersed with forest.

I am in the car with Bill, Tricia and Sarah, and we are driving to the Mosers' new home in Missouri after a weeklong road trip that included a weekend retreat in Pennsylvania with a group of Mennonites and Amish discussing how to help people assimilate more successfully into the faith, a stop at the Amish Mennonite Cultural Center in Berlin, Ohio, and a visit to two plain Christian communities in Kentucky. It is about 11 o'clock at night when we pull up to the house the Mosers are renting—a three-bedroom ranch with a two-car garage and basement, perched along a highway. I can't help but feel startled to see three black cars parked in the driveway.

I time travel back to 1998, when I first pulled into the Moser driveway in Ovid and saw a black horse carriage parked there. Somehow I am almost more shaken by seeing the cars than I was when I saw the buggy, I suppose because I had come to see the horse and buggy as emblematic of what Bill and Tricia and their family stood for—which is, of course, a central purpose of the horse and buggy in the plain cultures, and is a testament to the power of that symbol, that device, if I can call it that.

The family moved here to join an Amish-Mennonite community, a religious denomination that adheres to the same statement of belief, the 18 Articles of Faith, that their Old Order Amish community adhered to, but their new church differs in important ways. Central for the Mosers, services are in English, though Pennsylvania German dialect remains a part of their day-to-day because nearly all of the congregation members are ex-Amish—but they switch to English when the Mosers are in the conversation. For Bill and Tricia in particular (their children are all fluent in Pennsylvania German), the absence of German language in the church service removes what became the source of so many of their struggles during their life as Old Order Amish.

The other big change is that church members can drive cars. Horses and buggies are no longer a mandatory part of their lives, although their youngest son, Jacob, the family's biggest animal lover, did insist on moving his horse to Missouri.

As for attire in their new church, the Mosers still dress, for the most part, as they did in Marion. Tricia and Sarah still wear prairie-style dresses and white caps. Bill still has a beard and longish hair and wears plain pants and shirts. There is, however, a change in matter of degree. Bill's beard is more trimmed, his hair somewhat shorter, more kept. Bill concedes that there is more an element of fashion awareness among Amish-Mennonite girls than what Sarah grew up with in Marion.

One thing I've been struck by during the course of this project is that the Mosers, though Amish, though functioning until just recently in a plain culture that gets around by horse and buggy, are perhaps the busiest people I know, and their house always has a sense of "doing" about it—stuff lying here and there that tells of somebody's latest project, and this mid-November evening is no different. We open the front door, hauling luggage from the road trip, and step into a living room a-jumble with camping and hunting gear. Camouflage backpacks, boots, coats, and sleeping bags in stuff-sacks are stacked in corners, piled on chairs. Deer rifles—bolt action rifles with scopes—lean against the wall.

The gear is gathered for Matthew and Aaron's hunting trip; they're scheduled to leave in two days. The boys are heading out in a group of about eight to hunt deer. Pulling a horse trailer, they will drive to a forest not far away and then pack in with the horses to set camp. A few years ago, eldest son Tristan did similar trips in Montana, hunting elk in the mountains, so he no doubt lent advice.

The mom, the dad, the six grown children, they are all moving about the small living room and dining room, dropping luggage from the weeklong road trip, putting things away, stepping around backpacks and camping gear and guns and all talking. The boys are curious about who was seen on the road trip, and they want an update. Who is now married? Who is doing well? Who is living where? Who has moved from one community to another? Who has not moved from one community to another? The why of the move. The why of the non-move. This conversation is the endless soundtrack to the lives I have seen, an endless stream of Amish names and a thousand dramas invoking community and faith and family.

In the morning, Bill and the four oldest boys head to work. Bill, Tristan and Matthew work at a cabinet shop, jobs they found with a church member's company—arranged to support the family's transition. Timothy works at the truss-building shop that the family is buying, and Aaron works with a metal roof installer, also a business owned by a church member. I'm reminded again of the support the Anabaptist communities provide members when it comes to finding work, starting businesses, just making a living. Tricia, Sarah and Jacob are home, and as I enter the kitchen, Tricia offers me homemade granola, homemade yogurt and family-harvested and canned blueberries for breakfast.

Tricia and Sarah are busy, working in the kitchen. Jacob heads out to the pole barn to milk the family's Jersey cow. Occasionally, randomly, spontaneously, Sarah starts to sing, brightening the space with a hymn sung in a clear, strong contralto. A few stanzas later, she abruptly stops. Some minutes later, a few more stanzas rise from her.

Tricia finishes dishes and checks voicemail on speaker-phone. "You have sixteen new messages," the message service voice says, and one by one, Tricia clicks through them. The voice of Bill's mom, saying she is doing well after her shoulder surgery, the voice of somebody from church giving event information, the voices of friends from distant states wanting to connect, others reaching out for information. It's more of the Amish soundtrack, that constantly humming, tightly connected 300,000-person community off the radar of mainstream America.

I head out for the day and drive around the Mosers' new town. I see several signs related to Christianity. One sign says, "Atheism is a temporary condition." Another says the classic, "Are you prepared to meet thy God?" Bill tells me later that it is a Mennonite custom to erect signs with scripture at home.

This is Bible Belt country, and I see that Baptist churches abound. I consider the *Martyrs Mirror* and its many, many, many stories of people who believed in infant baptism killing people who believed infant baptism was wrong. How many of the people here know of that history? I'm thinking very few. And who would really care even if they did know—after all, the persecutions happened 400 or 500 years ago. Yet, in nearly every Amish and Mennonite home, that history is kept alive with one of the most important books in their culture, and that culture exists side by side with Bible Belt culture.

At the end of the workday, the Moser men come home. They are tired. The sons have been on their feet all day, and you can sense their fatigue as they clear living room chairs of camping gear and settle in. They talk about the day. They occasionally reference Jesus. Timothy picks up three deer-rifle bullets. They softly click as he absent-mindedly rolls them around in his hand like one might play with, say, a few pens.

As the men talk in the living room, Tricia and Sarah fix dinner. Home-canned corn, meatloaf with a barbeque sauce baked on top, mashed potatoes, coffee with cream from the Jersey cow, and for dessert, a chocolate cake with a warm chocolate sauce. At dinner we talk about the Pennsylvania conference again, who was there, what was the latest news on each. Timothy in particular wants the details of his family's latest road trip through the land of Amish, Mennonite and plain people.

After dinner, the table is cleaned, and I ask Bill to pull out his family's copy of the *Martyrs Mirror*. The book is so thick, I don't know where to begin, and I ask Bill about some interesting parts. "There seemed to be a lot of killings around 1528," he says. We flip to a page and the first thing I read is an account of a woman who refuses to renounce adult baptism, so she is tied to a stake and an executioner—supported by the official Christian church and government—calmly strangles her and then lights a fire beneath her. I know it happened 500 years ago, but it feels so vivid, not something from a bad black and white film or a scene from a historical fantasy novel, but something real that happened to a real woman. As the author intended, the impact travels through time, from that moment to me. It's more than I'm up for. I close the book.

We sit at the table and chat. I want to know about how the kids feel about Caneyville, the plain community we visited in Kentucky, a community that lives lower on the technology scale than most Amish communities. I concede I was somewhat charmed by the place and the people I met there—a beautiful mountain valley, intelligent people committed to their faith and way of life. It felt so safely embracing to me, like a giant terrarium where a family could thrive. So I'm surprised when some of the boys don't seem enthused about the idea of moving there if given the choice. Tristan and Sarah seem to be the only ones who would be maybe willing to try it.

Some of the objections seem small to me. The issue of the outhouse comes up again. I say it doesn't seem that bad to me. Try it at the end of August, after a hundred days of Kentucky heat, somebody says. I'm especially surprised when Jacob bluntly sums up his view: "What's the point?" The question is so surprising to me because, in a sense, the same could be asked of any technology boundary all along the line.

Other issues seem larger and get to the point of life choices. To be a man there, you would either farm, work in the wood-stove factory or in the jam factory. The Moser boys seemed to think that the benefits the community offered did not make up for the limited choices in avocation. The conversation is another reminder that America's culture of plain communities is not one simple unified, monolithic thing, but more a rainbow of communities and cultures that divide along a million different fracture lines.

But as mentioned, the Mosers are a busy family, and though Bill, Tricia, Sarah and Tristan are just back from a multi-day road trip, they are traveling again this coming weekend, this time to Arkansas because a church there has asked the Moser children, known as good singers, to come and help with some choral instruction. To prepare, tonight the children are pulling together their song list, selecting titles, practicing songs, keeping some, rejecting others.

The weekend will be just prior to Thanksgiving, so they want a theme of thanks woven through the choices. One song I like, "Every Day Is a Beautiful Day." The children are sitting around the dining room table. Timothy picks up the bass part. Sarah comes in with her contralto. Jacob has the tenor, but sometimes a baritone. Tristan is also a tenor, and is also the choir director. He marks time with his hand, making the classic motions for his siblings to follow, to stay on track. Jacob says why get caught up in all of that—the technicalities. "Just sing it, and if it sounds good, that's fine."

Tristan looks at him. The oldest brother assessing the youngest brother. "Yeah, when the timing is right and the notes are right it sounds good," he says.

It's good banter. It's all fun tension. But it's also a beautiful moment of a family of grown children sitting together on a Wednesday night in November, singing, and I can't help but consider the life choices the Mosers made to bring their family to this point. Nobody is cloistered away in a dark basement bedroom playing video games hour after hour while tossing back Monster drinks and Doritos. So much seems brought into focus at this moment.

The singing reminds me of a story Bill told me about the family's final night in Marion before they left the Old Order Amish and moved here. The truck was packed, and the Mosers were going to pull out at 5 a.m. A family with whom they were close stayed that evening after the truck was loaded and hung around. Several of the kids' friends came by, many boys and young men in particular, since the Mosers have five boys. They gathered close in the Mosers' living room, talked, sang songs. And one song in particular stood out, "Brothers in Christ." Bill said hearing that song at that moment, after a long and physical day of packing, just hours before leaving the horse-and-buggy life they had worked at for fifteen years, just hours from leaving the friends and families they had raised their children with, was one of the most potent moments of his life.

I ask the Moser children about the song. I ask them to sing it.

So they sing it. The words are simple, plain. "I've known you since we were little. I am by you. You are by me ..." The message is an "I got your back" sort of thing. To me, the song is nicely sung. But when they are done singing, the Moser children are not satisfied with the result. They talk it through, who needs to do what to make the song come together.

The children had tried to find the sheet music to "Brothers in Christ" and contacted the people who wrote it. The people said there is no sheet music. The song just gets learned and passed along. In that way it shares something with the songs in *The Ausbund*, the universal Amish songbook that has words to songs, but no musical notation; the tunes live only in people's minds, spreading only person to person in the most ancient human way. The backstory about the song "Brothers in Christ" adds potency and richness, that a song could exist so ephemerally, beyond technology, beyond even the technology of paper. This fact seems to embody so much of the Amish way, a trusting of human-scale interaction, things that live only in the realm of spirituality and faith, brotherhood and community and thought.

At some point I ask Bill if he regrets having worked so long and so hard—fifteen years—to make the Amish lifestyle work. No, he doesn't regret leaving mainstream America for a moment. "I didn't want to die always wondering, What if I had done something else? I did the something else," he says.

......

Some months later, during final reviews of this book's manuscript, Bill wrote me a note. He asked that we include this brief paragraph as a parting statement.

"The same desire and longing I identified with in the rock/rebellion anti-establishment culture during my early twenties I have found in Christian culture and especially in Anabaptist groups who believe in living out kingdom Christianity. I have escaped from the kingdoms of this world into God's kingdom, expressed and lived out in church community."—*Bill Moser*

......

.

{WITH GRATITUDE}

I wish to express thanks and great gratitude to the Moser family—Bill, Tricia, Tristan, Timothy, Aaron, Sarah, Matthew, Jacob and Grandma Joyce—for their willingness to share their story with the broader world. Also, deep thanks to my own family, my wife, Linda, and my children—Wyatt, Audrey, Cara, Trevor and daughter-in-law Jen Superson—and step-father George Gottschalk for their support and thoughts and direction. A giant thank-you to Deborah Wyatt Fellows, who has given me the opportunity to serve as editor of *Traverse, Northern Michigan's Magazine,* and to write about a place and life I love. An extra special thanks to Kirt Manecke for ongoing advice and encouragement. Huge thanks to Bob Wilcox for his wonderful book design and Caroline "C.D." Dahlquist for her magnificent proofreading skills. A warm thank-you to Lissa Edwards for her ongoing enthusiasm. And thanks to friends and family who took a spin through various drafts and offered feedback ... Dave Waskin, Heather Hollick, Chris and Debbie Olson, Lisa Confer, Paul Kolak, Brian Ursu, Andy (Bennett) Sullivan, Bob Dotson, Brittany Morton, Alex Werder, Jonathan Manuel Romero Robles. And of course, great gratitude to the people of the Amish and plain communities who allowed me into their homes to discuss their faith and ways ... Joni and Barbara Mast of Gladwin, Michigan, Alfred and Martha Gingerich of Manton, Michigan, Freeman and Wilma Troyer, formerly of Marion, Michigan, Bryce and Eloise Geiser of Caneyville, Kentucky. And thanks to Steve Troyer of Millersburg, Ohio, for a personal tour of the grand historical mural—the Behalt Cyclorama—at the Amish Mennonite Heritage Center in Berlin, Ohio. And thanks to Rev. William Lindholm, who was willing to dig deep into his memory to re-tell his story of the Supreme Court Amish education case in which he played such an important role.—*Jeff Smith*

{*ABOUT THE AUTHOR*}

Jeff Smith is a journalist and editor who has written extensively about the environment, outdoors and lifestyle during the course of his 30-plus year career. He currently edits *Traverse, Northern Michigan's Magazine*, an award-winning monthly regional publication focused on life near the shores of the Great Lakes. In his previous position, Jeff wrote for nearly a decade about federal and state environmental law and policy related to the world of hazardous and low-level radioactive waste.

Jeff first wrote about his lifelong friends the Mosers during the economic crash of 2008. The magazine story folded into the national conversation about people looking for simpler and more meaningful ways to live balanced and fulfilled lives. Jeff wondered what perspective the Mosers, who had left one of America's wealthiest communities to become horse-and-buggy Amish, could bring to that conversation.

The book *Becoming Amish* grew from his belief that, though few modern families would ever become Amish, there were many aspects of the Amish life that could inform today's families as they contemplated shaping more intentional lives. He also saw that the Mosers, as people who grew up in modern, everyday America, brought unique perspective to the topic because they were both insiders and outsiders in the Amish world, and their observations would resonate with their contemporary peers.

Jeff and his wife Linda have four children and live in Cedar, Michigan, near northern Lake Michigan and the Sleeping Bear Dunes National Lakeshore. In his spare time, Jeff kayaks, canoes, cycles, hikes, cross-country skis, snowshoes and attempts to grow vegetables.—*Jeff Smith*

Made in the USA
Monee, IL
28 July 2022

10406136R10152